Jesus Driven Life

Jesus Driven Life

A rough guide to the Sermon on the Mount

By Gerard Kelly

With additional material by Nick Shepherd and Peter Phillips

MILTON KEYNES ● COLORADO SPRINGS
HYDERABAD

First published as Humanifesto in 2001 by Spring Harvest Publishing Divison
and Paternoster Lifestyle. Reprinted 2009 as Jesus Driven Life

15 14 13 12 11 10 09   7 6 5 4 3 2 1

9 Holdom Avenue, Bletchley, Milton Keynes, Bucks, MK1 1QR, UK
1820 Jet Stream Drive, Colorado Springs, CO 80921, USA
OM Authentic Media, Medchal Road, Jeedimetla Village, Secunderabad 500 055, A.P., India
www.authenticmedia.co.uk

Authentic Media is a division of IBS-STL U.K., limited by guarantee, with its Registered Office at
Kingstown Broadway, Carlisle, Cumbria CA3 0HA. Registered in England & Wales No. 1216232.
Registered charity 270162

British Library Cataloguing in Publication Data
A catalogue record for this book is available from the British Library

ISBN 978-1-85078-839-3

Print Management by Adare
Printed and bound in the UK by J F Print Ltd, Sparkford, Somerset.

Contents

Acknowledgements vii
Foreword. ix
Introduction xi

DISTRICT 1: CENTRAL
The City at the Heart of the City 1
Tourist Information Panel One 20
Tourist Information Panel Two 21

DISTRICT 2: LEGAL
The Old Court Buildings. 22
Tourist Information Panel Three 43
Tourist Information Panel Four 44

DISTRICT 3: SPIRITUAL
A River Runs Through It. 45
Tourist Information Panel Five 65
Tourist Information Panel Six 66

DISTRICT 4: FINANCIAL
Of Rust and Trust 67
Tourist Information Panel Seven 84
Tourist Information Panel Eight 85

DISTRICT 5: FRUITFUL
The Artisan Quarter. 87

References 104

Acknowledgements

Big thanks to Mark Finnie, Ali Hull and all at Authentic for believing in this book and bringing this new edition to birth. Thanks, also, to Pete Phillips and Nick Shepherd for the use of their added study material. And my special thanks to Chrissie, my partner in life and mission and to Joe, Aaron, Anna and Jake for their friendship, input and inspiration.

This book is dedicated with gratitude and affection to Richard A. Russell, whose teaching series on the Sermon on the Mount at St Matthews in Bath set a fire in my head and heart that burns to this day. It was through the style and content of Richard's teaching that I first came to see Christ's words as a manifesto for humanity. That I am still, twenty years later, exploring that thrilling discovery is a mark of the impact Richard has had. Thank you.

Foreword

I often get asked to review new books. Many of them are good and just sometimes they are excellent. This book is an excellent introduction to the Sermon on the Mount and deserves to be widely read. Punchy, and well written, focused on practical contemporary application, it will both challenge and encourage its readers.

Fran Beckett
Chief Executive of Shaftesbury and Chair of REBUILD

If you come any day between March and November, you will find crowds of men, women and children wandering around, just gazing in amazement. They come from all over the world. Why? Because this is one of the wonders of the world. *The Dean of Salisbury cathedral*[1]

And the Alps! They are sufficient reason alone for visiting Switzerland. The countryside is visually stunning. Breathtaking views inspire peace and tranquillity and provide many sporting opportunities for the more adventurous. ... Then there's the picturesque capital, Berne, that looks more like a museum piece than a seat of power. *Switzerland – The Lonely Planet Guide*[2]

INTRODUCTION

If the teachings of Jesus were an architectural tour, the Sermon on the Mount would be a glorious cathedral. If they were a foreign country, this hillside homily would be its capital city. For many people this is the entry point into the teachings of the New Testament. For those seeking to make sense of their lives, these words have been one of the world's most popular destinations since the moment they were first uttered. Some of history's greatest spiritual travellers have found strength and inspiration in this territory. Of those who have visited, many have chosen to stay. There are other accounts of the life and teachings of Jesus – other stories and other things he said and did – but the whole teaching of Jesus can in some senses be explored from the vantage point of this one sermon. As Paris is to France and Athens to ancient Greece, so is this Sermon to the life and work of Christ. If you're going to explore the country, this is a very good place to start.

The exploration of the Sermon on the Mount contained here will take the form of a travel guide. It is one tourist telling another where to find life. It is practical, but also personal: reflecting the accents of my own pilgrimage through this text. It considers the Sermon on the Mount, recorded in Chapters 5, 6 and 7 of Matthew's gospel, as a city to be explored: an ancient terrain of streets and stone, with monuments that have been visited by millions, and views that are known the world over. The city is set out, for our purposes, in five separate districts. In each of these we will explore the text in terms of between four and six 'Sites'- brief collections of verses worthy of examination and attention.

A WORD ABOUT WHAT THIS GUIDEBOOK IS, AND IS NOT

We have subtitled this book a rough guide to the Sermon on the Mount for good reason. It is an introductory guide, not an exhaustive commentary. Strictly speaking, it is not a commentary at all, being more impressionistic and intuitive than expository. I have written in much the same way as I would if I was asked to write a book about France. My reason for writing would not be that I know all there is to know about France, but that I have lived in France, I have travelled in France, and I love France. The same is true of the Sermon on the Mount. I write about these words because, like many others, I have tried for many years to live in them. I write because I have 'travelled' in them, exploring and examining their many levels of meaning. And I write because I love these words. The power that is wrapped up in these sayings of Jesus is not an academic power. It is not something to be dissected, pinned to a board and projected onto a lecture-room screen. It is an experienced power, a lived power. These words are mysterious and magnetic, intriguing and inspiring. Since my teenage years, I have by turns been puzzled, enthralled, challenged, affirmed and 'blessed' by these words. I love them most of all because even after nearly three decades of exploration, I still don't understand the half of them. Time and time again, I find myself drawn back to this teaching – and time and time again I am surprised. Equally, if I was writing about France, it would not be to save you the bother of visiting for yourself. Far from it – I would urge you, at every turn, to do so. I would present France to you as a vast territory to be explored. I would freely admit to you that there is more to be discovered of France than I know or could ever know. And I would hold out the hope that you, encouraged by my jottings to visit for yourself, would find out things that I had completely missed.

The purpose of the guide is to point out the headlines and highlights of the territory. Just as every major city can be

known by its key monuments and neighbourhoods – think of the Sydney Opera House and the Seattle Space Needle, of London's Albert Hall or New York's Empire State Building – so the Sermon on the Mount has themes and landmarks that break the skyline and cry out for attention. Those who stay longer and get to know the detail – who can name not only the main streets but the back alleys that join them – will discover how much more there is to explore beyond the well-known sights. But for the new visitor, the tourist who wants to get to know the area, it is the well-known monuments that must be explored first. If this guide does nothing else, it will at least tell you where to start looking.

Like any guidebook, this journey through the Sermon on the Mount has its own limitations. There will be places in which I have chosen to linger where you would much rather move on quickly to consider the next site. There will be other places we rush through like tourists doing Europe in a week, where you would rather stay and drink in the riches and atmosphere. The choices of sites to explore, as well as the exploration made, are subjective. At each stop, there is only so much that can be said before the tour moves on. My only advice when such frustrations arise is that you follow your instincts, and linger longer on your own initiative. Let the tour party rush to where they will: if you have found a place in this Sermon you would like to stay for a while, then stay! Take as many pictures as you want, jot down your impressions – or just let the text speak to you down the ages. Like thousands who have gone before, you may find a favourite spot to which you are drawn back time and again. This is as it should be. There are phrases in this sermon in which you could live unmoving for a lifetime – and still not explore to the limit. Blessed are the tourists who know when to stop, for they shall see the sights their tour guides miss. There are a number of features in the layout of this guide that you will need to be aware of to get the most out of it.

THE DISTRICTS

There are five of these, together covering Chapters 5 to 7 of Matthew's Gospel. They are not equal in length but are thematic, representing the core sections or themes of the Sermon. They are sequential however, dealing with the text as Matthew gives it. There are many reasons for this, but the best is that it is practical and easy to follow. If you want to break off from the tour and take some other route, covering the material in a different order, please do so. But the tour itself will progress verse by verse. When you want to rejoin it, just look for the gaggle of camera-clickers led by the fat guy with the little yellow flag. Where each of the five districts is introduced, there is information covering the whole of that section of the Sermon. This overview includes:

■ **Orientation and information**: introducing the district and setting it in its wider context.

■ **Highlights**: letting you know what is to come in the sites to be visited.

THE SITES

Within each of these districts, the text has been divided into 4 to 6 sites, each of which we will visit for 1200 words or so. At each site, our visit will follow the same pattern, offering an exploration that includes:

■ **Location:** the exact verses under consideration, as given in the New International Version.

■ **Landmarks:** a few words in summary of the main thrust of these verses.

■ **What to see:** a thematic exploration of the passage in question.

■ **What to do:** some suggestions for action and response.

■ **Places to stay:** a brief prayer, quote or meditation with which to linger for a few moments.

■ **Retro-tour:** the same passage as given in the Authorised [King James] Version.

You may wonder why the very old-fashioned language of the Authorised Version of the Bible has been included in this text – reproduced at each site on the panel marked Retro-tour. There is a very good reason for this inclusion. The power of this text and the richness of this territory to all those willing to visit it do not only come from the content and context of the Sermon itself. They come also from history: from the fact that for twenty centuries these words have inspired, uplifted, instructed and challenged women and men. For four hundred of those years, in the English-speaking world, it has been in the Authorised Version that the Sermon has been known and explored. When you watch Baz Luhrmann's exotic film of *Romeo and Juliet*, you are moved in part by the knowledge that this love story, and the rich and poetic language with which it is expressed, have enthralled young lovers for four centuries. Luhrmann's central device – to keep the old language but make everything around it new – has remarkable power: a power that a modernisation of the text would almost certainly lose. The Bible is not Shakespeare, and I am not Baz Luhrmann, but the principle is the same. The inclusion of these ancient phrases in this

guide reminds us of the deep and colourful provenance of the sites we are exploring. The Sermon on the Mount is not a deserted city, perfectly preserved for us in the pristine condition in which Jesus left it. It is a lived-in city, a territory in which generation upon generation have made their home and gone about their lives. The greatest minds in our history have spent time in this place, and some of the deepest channels of our culture have been carved here. Many proverbs in our language began their life as postcards from the Sermon on the Mount. It is an important aspect of our tour to ask not only what these words meant when first spoken, but also what they have meant since, as whole civilisations have been built up, or brought to their knees, by their power. Like stone steps warped and worn down by the feet of centuries passing over them, the path to the Sermon on the Mount is well-trodden. At every point, thousands of pilgrims before us have walked, watched, knelt, reflected and absorbed these words. This is a historic site of the highest order.

THE HELP FILES

In addition to the district overviews and site visits, there will also appear from time to time in the text Tourist Information Panels. These offer background and technical information which is helpful to the overall understanding of the Sermon on the Mount, but which does not fit neatly into any single site visit. Tackling questions of language, context and customs, these panels help to situate the Sermon in its

historical and cultural setting – and may just add to your appreciation of it.

There are also occasional Subway Stations, which suggest Old Testament passages and references relevant to the verses under consideration. The Old Testament runs beneath the Sermon on the Mount much in the way that an underground rail system or Metro runs under many of the world's major cities. At times it is all but invisible, but its hidden tracks and tunnels form a networked structure to the text, connecting key verses with each other and with parallel passages elsewhere in the teachings of Jesus. In most cases, time and space do not allow us to detour into a full exploration of the Old Testament allusions in the Sermon. But simply reading these additional texts throws new light on the depths and richness of the mind of Christ. It is one of the tragedies of the modern era that our disdain for past traditions has devalued the Old Testament witness for us. As a result we are unaware of just how often Jesus was citing ancient texts – either by allusion or by direct quotation. Had Jesus been on *Who Wants to be A Millionaire?* he would never have got an Old Testament question wrong. These were texts he knew and loved, and

the Sermon on the Mount is full of them. It is possible to ignore these references, and continue exploring the terrain at surface level – but those who take the trouble to dig deep will find the effort richly rewarded; discovering a whole world of content and connections to add to the abundance of the Sermon.

There is also an Index, at the end of the tour. This gives page references for each verse of the Sermon, and also tells you where to find key words and themes. Lastly, there is a Notes section in support of the references and quotes used on the tour. This is not there just to prove we didn't invent them, but also to suggest some routes for future tours. A bibliography is also included. This is not a comprehensive reading list – but a selection of links which offer a good place to start.

DISTRICT 1: CENTRAL
The City at the Heart of the City

Matthew 5:1-16

Orientation and information

Imagine a city built on the side of a mountain. Visible for miles around, it offers an unforgettable and unmistakable image. At the city's heart, streets and alleys climb the steep slopes that rise up from the earth like a wedding cake. The windows of the upper houses look out over the roofs of those below as buildings rise in stepped neatness. At the very top, a temple or cathedral stands – or perhaps a statue or Telecom tower – giving to the cityscape an instantly recognisable silhouette. The Mont St Michel, on the border of Normandy and Brittany in France, is one such place. More than just an abbey, it is a whole town built on a hill that rises unexpectedly from the flat tidal plains of the bay. The distinct outline of the community, rising to a point at the very tip of the Abbey's highest spire, has been transmitted on post-cards, photographs and car-stickers to every corner of the world. It is an unforgettable site, visible on a clear day from miles out at sea as well as from Avranches and other towns inland. Considered a holy place from time immemorial, the mount stands out as a key landmark of the north-western coast of Europe.

This is the kind of physical image that the Sermon on the Mount, in literary terms, aspires to. This is the manifesto of Jesus: his response to the aspirations and expectations of the Hebrew people and at the same time his voice into every age and culture. These had to be memorable words, principles that would leave such a unique and unmistakable silhouette in the minds of all who came across them, that they would without hesitation be able to point and say 'this is the message of Christ.'

Even within the New Testament canon – a body of literature rich in its significance and depth – the Sermon on the Mount stands out. It is a key landmark and more: a place of pilgrimage, an unmistakable silhouette; a site to which visitors are drawn back time and time again. Within the Sermon, the 'district' that stands out as the heart of the enterprise – that sets the tone for the rest – is the passage from verse 1 to 16 of chapter 5: the sayings known as the Beatitudes and the call to be the world's salt and light. This is the monument at the centre of the city from which the whole has earned its name and fame. These are the principles that the remainder of the sermon will explore. It is hard to think of a body of sayings that more perfectly capture the thoughts of Jesus, or that have more deeply inspired the generations that have chosen to follow him. Whole movements in human history have been sparked by the meanings of these words. Challenging and mysterious, the Beatitudes are impossible to fully explain – but impossible to entirely ignore. Visitors to the Sermon on the Mount are drawn into the enigma of these verses just as surely as tourists in Paris will find themselves, sooner or later, staring up at the Eiffel Tower. You will never understand New York until you have felt the feelings of an immigrant, approaching by ship, when the Statue of Liberty first comes into view. So, too, you will miss the deeper sense and power of the Sermon unless you take the time to 'live in' this key passage. As Mecca is the heart of Islam, this text is the heart of the Christian faith.

HIGHLIGHTS

- The King of the Hill
- Inheritance facts
- We want to see cheeses
- What will the neighbours say?
- Take the taste test
- Strike a light!

---

1. THE KING OF THE HILL

Location *Matthew 5:1-2.* Now when he saw the crowds, he went up on a mountainside and sat down. His disciples came to him, and he began to teach them...

Landmarks Those who have ears to hear come together, to glean what they can from the Messiah's manifesto.

What to see If you cross the central plains of America, or drive from the northern coastlands of France across Belgium and into Holland, you can pass through mile upon mile of terrain without so much as a gentle gradient. There are whole regions with barely a hill to skateboard down, let alone ski-slopes and mountain ranges. In these lands of flatness, straight roads and canals cut endlessly across geometric fields, and cars travel much as crows fly. No image could stand in more stark contrast to that of the land of Israel at the time of Jesus. A harsh terrain of steep rocky slopes, criss-crossed with valleys and narrow passes, Israel was a nation bounded and defined by its mountains. Even the simplest journey from city to city could be arduous – detoured and delayed by the dangers of mountain travel. For the people of this hill-strewn landscape, the proud and resilient Hebrews born of the seed of Abraham, mountains held a central place in both mythology and history. From the first journeys of Abraham and the call of Moses; through the giving of the law and the trials and triumphs of the prophets; to the daily expectation of Messiah's coming, mountains spoke of majesty and power; of the deep mysteries of God, of the presence of the untouchable Creator. Throughout the literature of Israel, the mountainous landscape persists as both sacred ['the mountain of God'] and scary ['the valley of the shadow of death'].

When Jesus climbed the mountainside and sat down to teach, his disciples knew that what would follow would be important to them. The very foundations of the nation of Israel were laid when Moses did the same. It is impossible to know for sure whether Matthew is recording a single Sermon delivered at one sitting, or a series of discourses given over several days. It may be, as some scholars claim, that he has gathered the significant words of Jesus from a variety of settings and arranged them around one, resonant memory. His purpose seems clear – he was creating a catechism; a discipleship curriculum for the early church. There is compelling evidence that where Luke came to his task as a historian, Matthew's first concern is as a teacher. The Sermon on the Mount is the first of four 'closely ordered collections'[3] of the teachings of Jesus in Matthew[4]; teaching which is scattered widely in Luke.[5]

But whichever of these is the case, the hillside discourse carries within itself the very foundations of the Christian faith. This is Jesus' own Alpha course: the indispensable basics on which the

teachings of the Church would be built for centuries to come. He has seen the crowd – he knows that the time has come to set out his stall. He begins by addressing his close followers, the tiny band of friends who have already begun to look to him for leadership. But he must surely know that the crowds will not be far behind; that as his teaching begins, onlookers will gather and an ad hoc congregation will grow. From the outset it is clear that this is public teaching: declared truth. Jesus has words to offer to all who have ears to hear – his friends first, then the gathered throng, then those who will come later, who may even listen over a chasm twenty centuries wide.

That these words have survived for as long as they have; that they have inspired millions and shaped history; that they have resisted every effort to reduce them to empty religion or elevate them to archaic law; these are the measures of the effectiveness with which the manifesto is delivered.

No editor in his right mind would ignore a press conference called by Jesus. When the Creator of the universe takes time out to sit on a hillside and talk, knowing full well that the ears of the world are listening – the equivalent of CNN, the BBC and a hundred other stations competing to catch every sound-bite – you can be sure that what he has to say will carry weight. These are measured words, every sentence weighed and tested by the wisest of all minds. If we know

What to do

To take time to study the Sermon on the Mount is to follow in the footsteps of generations spread over two millennia. It is an historic journey; by reputation a life-changing quest. But how can the journey be made meaningful in today's over-busy culture? Here are three simple ideas:

■ **Begin a journal**. Set the approximate time frame within which you want to undertake this exploration, and make an appropriate commitment to the recording of your thoughts and reflections. This might be daily, weekly or monthly – or on some other basis with which you are comfortable. Make a serious commitment to keep this record alive – and ask God to speak to you through it: not only through the words you read or hear, but also through those you write.

■ **Find a mountain**. If you are fortunate enough to live in Wales or Scotland, or in the Alps or Rockies, this won't be difficult. In some flatter or more urban situations it may prove harder. But if there is a hill within visiting distance of your home, make appointments with yourself to visit it. Use whatever times you can muster to reflect on the thoughts the Sermon on the Mount is inspiring in you. Explore the message of the mountain in a mountainside setting. Open your heart and mind to hear from God – and invite the Messiah who climbed a hill to teach his friends to join you as you climb too.

■ **Digitise!** If you regularly use a PC or laptop, and have access to the internet, visit an on-line Bible site such as the *Bible Gateway* at http://www.gospelcom.net. From here you can download Matthew 5 to 7 in a range of versions and languages. Store these on your desktop and use the free moments of your day – few and far between though they may be – to browse the text. I visited the site recently and downloaded the Sermon on the Mount in the NIV and Authorised versions as well as in Young's Literal translation and the Louis Segond French translation. All of these – and especially the act of comparing them – have deepened my encounter with this text, and reading from the screen as well as on paper adds a new dimension. The *Bible Gateway* also offers word-search facilities by which you can explore the occurrences, throughout the Bible, of key words featured in Matthew 5 to 7.

If the Sermon on the Mount is as foundational a gospel text as we are claiming – and as time has shown it to be – then it deserves efforts such as these to aid and deepen our study. Christian disciples throughout history – from those who heard the words on the Galilean slopes to the millions who have had them translated into their languages – will bear witness that every investment in the study of these words has been rewarded a thousand times over.

Places to stay

The Sermon on the Mount is not a set of principles to be obeyed apart from identification with Jesus Christ. The Sermon on the Mount is a statement of the life we will live when the Holy Spirit is getting his way with us. *Oswald Chambers*[6]

If any one will piously and soberly consider the sermon which our Lord Jesus Christ spoke on the mount … I think he will find in it, so far as regards the highest morals, a perfect standard of the Christian life: and this we do not rashly venture to promise, but gather it from the very words of the Lord himself. For the sermon itself is brought to a close in such a way, that it is clear that there are in it all the precepts which go to mould the life. *Augustine of Hippo, 5th Century*

Father, Son and Holy Spirit – Maker, Messiah, motivator – be with me as I climb the paths of these texts. May the message of the mountain speak to me once more with fresh insight, renewed vigour and new power.

R E T R O - T O U R

And seeing the multitudes, he went up into a mountain: and when he was set, his disciples came unto him: And he opened his mouth, and taught them…

nothing else of Christ, we know that the message of the mountain is his heartbeat.

2. INHERITANCE FACTS

Location *Matthew 5:3-6.* Saying: 'Blessed are the poor in spirit, for theirs is the kingdom of heaven. Blessed are those who mourn, for they will be comforted. Blessed are the meek, for they will inherit the earth. Blessed are those who hunger and thirst for righteousness, for they will be filled.'

Landmarks The Beatitudes set out the values of an upside-down kingdom, in which Jesus identifies the targets of God's

blessing – who gets wet when the water pistol is fired. The good news of the kingdom is for all, excluding none.

What to see Who wants to be a millionaire? Who wants untold opportunity, unlimited wealth, unending happiness? By all accounts, we all do. From the foundation of the earth men and women have been locked into a search for self-fulfilment. 'In every state', Anatole France writes in *Penguin Island*, 'wealth is a sacred thing. In democracies it is the only sacred thing.'[7] Believing that happiness comes from 'money, sex and power',[8] we work for these goals, gamble for these goals, invest for these goals and risk all, if need be, for these goals. This is no twenty-first century phenomenon – it is the besetting problem of humankind. For all the diversity of cultures in geography and history, almost all see the 'winners' as the powerful, the rich and the sexually adept. And the yearning to be winners – to abandon the ranks of the 'have-nots' and take our place among the 'haves' – lies just below the surface of our many motivations. From domestic violence and the sex industry to the wars and empires that have killed and tortured millions, human history is a catalogue of the disasters that flow from our inability to deal with these appetites. And every true spiritual revival in history, from the Celts and Benedictines, via the Franciscans, Pietists and Methodists to this day, has been accompanied 'by a clear, bold response to the issues of money, sex and power.'[9]

So it is appropriate that the discourse in which Jesus will set out his plan for the reform and revival of humanity should begin with this implicit question 'Who are the winners?' For those who stood listening then, as for those who sit reading now, the question answers itself. The rich are winners. The powerful are winners. The sexually accomplished are winners. The realities of first century Palestine were not so very different from those of twenty-first century Hollywood. In either context, you need only look around to see the dominant and the opulent enjoying their glittering prizes. But the kingdom announcement of Jesus begins with a different claim. Here it is the poor in Spirit who are blessed; the meek who inherit; the bereaved who find true joy. Here it is those who are hungry – not those whose every hunger has been satisfied – who are on the path to self-fulfilment.

Like a solicitor reading the last will and testament of the recently deceased, Jesus names the beneficiaries of the Kingdom he announces. For the flamboyant Aunt Mabel, who might otherwise have expected to gain millions, there is nothing. But for young Cedric, the poor relative – the odd, forgotten cousin – there is good news. It is as though the blessing of God is a loaded water pistol. Not the low capacity, hand-held type, but a Ghostbusters Super-Soaker, with a backpack water reservoir linked up to a mains supply. God has watched over the suffering of humanity. He has seen his beautiful creation bruised and abused by the ravages of humankind's rebellion. He has waited for his moment, the pressure building all the time. And now Messiah has come – God's finger is on the trigger. The reign of God, like a fire-hydrant, is about to be released into the world. 'But who', Jesus asks us, 'will get wet first'? The answer is given in these phrases, known to us as the Beatitudes. It is amongst the poor and the dispossessed, those who suffer loss, the 'losers' in the culture wars, that God's kingdom will first come. It is to the dry ground that the rain will be drawn. Like a snooker table with one leg shorter than the rest, God's blessing has a bias towards the humble poor.

What to do

■ Consider this list of descriptive words: poor in Spirit; hungry; mourning; thirsty; meek. What kinds of images do these words bring to mind? What do the poor in Spirit look like? What are those who mourn doing? Who are the meek? How do the hungry and thirsty feel? Ask yourself, what kind of spirituality is built on these characteristics? How different is it from your own faith and practice?

■ If there is one place in twenty-first century culture where the characteristics Jesus describes are brought together, it is in a refugee camp. Here, the poor huddle, incapable of effecting change in their own lives. Here, every person has experienced suffering and loss in the recent past. Here, meekness is the unavoidable by-product of powerlessness. Here hunger and thirst are the daily fare. Find out all you can about the millions of refugees in today's world. Ask yourself what you might be able to do to help – and how their experience might shape and change your faith.

Places to stay

Our popular western culture insists that to be first is to be best and only those who excel are able to become icons of our age. All who do not attain this stage of excellence and domination are considered inadequate. It is here that the gospel kicks in and insists that inadequacy is the truth about us all. *Viv Thomas*[10]

Joy is not the same as happiness. Happiness depends on what happens. Happiness is a Porsche with a stereo stopping for you when it just started raining. Joy may rise in the midst of a thunderstorm with not a car to be seen. ... Happiness is the preserve of the lucky, the wealthy and the successful. Joy belongs to any who find it, and the poor seem to find more of it than most. *Mike Riddell*[11]

R E T R O - T O U R

Saying, Blessed are the poor in spirit: for theirs is the kingdom of heaven. Blessed are they that mourn: for they shall be comforted. Blessed are the meek: for they shall inherit the earth. Blessed are they which do hunger and thirst after righteousness: for they shall be filled.

Some have interpreted the Beatitudes as a list of new commandments to replace the old ten: a new framework of behavioural objectives for those out to impress their maker. Others see them as an impossible standard to show us how lost we are. But it seems more likely that they are a statement of intent and direction – an indication of the way God's blessing flows. This rings true for three reasons:

Firstly, because these statements carry the subversive nature of God's kingdom announcement. A new regime that leaves the old order in place: that leaves the bullies in power and the greedy with their unjust gains, and has nothing to say to the oppressed, is not good and is not news. The God of Israel – the God of Exodus – is the God who hears the cry of slaves and sends the cavalry. Only an upside-down kingdom will deliver true liberation.

Secondly because it is the humble poor who know their need of God. It is those who have nothing who know they need everything. The poor in spirit; the bereaved; the meek; the hungry and thirsty – these are the people who will look to God for salvation. What is the occasion that still, to this day, brings the agnostic, the atheist and the reprobate to church? – the funeral of a friend. Loss opens doors to the Spirit that gain and comfort have locked tight. There are moments in our lives when we look to the kingdom of heaven, when we turn our faces toward God. It is in these moments, more than any other, that he looks to catch our eye and bless us.

Thirdly, there is a bias to the poor because only in this can the Gospel announcement truly be for all. The principle is simple – the poor have no means of their own to become rich, nor the powerless to gain power. But the rich and powerful have within themselves the possibility of becoming poor. Salvation offered only to winners will by definition exclude many. Only salvation offered to losers – whether by circumstance or by choice – can be described as comprehensive. There is nothing you don't have that can bar you from entry to this kingdom – only the things you have might keep you out.

⊖ **S U B W A Y   M A P**

STATION
Isaiah 61:1-2 – an ancient promise that those who mourn would receive blessing and joy.

CONNECTIONS
Revelation 7:17 – a future promise of a day when every tear will be dried.

3. WE WANT TO SEE CHEESES...

Location *Matthew 5:7-9.* Blessed are the merciful, for they will be shown mercy. Blessed are the pure in heart, for they will see God. Blessed are the peacemakers, for they will be called sons of God.

Landmarks Being and doing are inseparably intertwined: inward transformation is expressed in outward actions;

the kingdom is what you are, and what you make of what you are.

What to see A piece of late twentieth century graffiti summed up the philosophical history of the world in these words:

To do is to be – *Rousseau*

To be is to do – *Sartre*

Doobedoobedoobedoo… – *Sinatra*[12]

Of the three, Sinatra was the closest to the truth. Being and doing are inextricably woven together in the creation – they are the two threads from which the pattern of humanity is made. Like inseparable partners, they dance so closely together in our lives that it is impossible to see which is leading. Any attempt to separate the two – to reduce human complexity to statements of cause and effect – fails to ring true with reality. Who you are and how you are, are the two sides of one coin; two ways of looking at identity. This is a theme that Jesus will explore later, looking at words and deeds and at trees and fruit, but here it is reflected in the second group of Beatitudes. The emphasis seems to shift – from 'being' poor, bereaved, meek and hungry to the 'doing' of mercy, peacemaking and purity of heart. Where the early Beatitudes could legitimately be seen as passive, describing a condition over which the subject may have little or no control, these later statements are proactive. It is a choice to show mercy, to make peace, to pursue

purity of heart. Though it is open to some, as we have seen, to become poor, meek or hungry by choice, for many these are conditions thrust upon us. Mercy, peacemaking and purity, by contrast, are always chosen.

In taking this direction, Jesus is dealing with some of the deepest questions of human experience, and revealing the fullness of the kingdom vision. He strikes out the very possibility of separating being from doing. There are two opposite groups who make this separation – the hyper-religious and the hyper-liberal. The religious – represented in the days of Jesus by the teachers of the Law – see only doing as important. It is what you do that pleases or displeases God. Behaviour is everything, intention nothing. Do the right thing, and God will honour you – no matter what conflicting sentiments you harbour. This is the philosophy described elsewhere by Jesus as the life of the white-washed tomb. But the opposite extreme, in which behaviour doesn't matter at all and only intention counts, is equally distorted. Those who say that as long as you mean well, as long as your heart is in the right place, it doesn't matter what you do, are also in the wrong.

Jesus resolves these extremes by using 'being' and 'doing' interchangeably. Those who show mercy are merciful; those who make peace are peacemakers. God looks to the heart, but he looks also to the actions that flow from it. There is a deep mystery here, which lies at the core

What to do

■ Reflect on what it has meant for you to experience mercy in your life. Where have you received not what you deserved, but what love dictated? Ask yourself what it will mean to show such mercy to those around you: perhaps especially those you think might deserve some other response!

■ Consider what the word purity means in its deepest sense. Think of pure water, of pure air, of a pure diamond. Ask yourself what it might mean for you to seek such purity in all your being and doing.

■ Meditate on what the idea of peace has meant in your life. Think of rest; of freedom from oppression and violence; of a place and time in which you are able to be yourself – in which you sense that you are at one with the Creator and his creation. Ask yourself what it might take to make such peace in the world around you.

Father, giving thanks for your mercy, I commit myself to being merciful.

Jesus, having seen and received your purity, I commit myself to purity of heart.

Sprit, having known and loved your peace, I offer myself as a peacemaker in your world.

of the human condition. We are organic creatures, not robots, and in the organic world what the seed is and what it does are intertwined. To describe the process by which an apple-seed produces apples is to state both what it is and what it does. The temptation in the face of this mystery is to go in one of two directions: to seek behaviour that is super-human, setting us above our worldly peers, or to accept behaviour that is sub-human, responding to the animal in us all. The teaching of Jesus, by contrast, is not there to deliver us from the mess and mystery of the human condition, but to make sense of it.

In these Beatitudes, Jesus is letting us know that what will follow – the more extensive exploration of the 'how-to' of these great principles – will speak to us equally and inseparably of both being and doing. There is no list of desired behaviours which can be 'done' without a transformation of being. But neither is there any inner transformation on offer that will not show itself in changed behaviour. Which paper do citizens of this kingdom carry – a job description or a birth certificate? The answer is both and either one without the other is sub-Christian.

Places to stay

Since wars begin in the minds of men, it is in the minds of men that the defence of peace must be constructed. *The UNESCO Constitution*[13]

Every small deed of tending the garden is an act of worship. It is our bowed knee to the One who created the garden and calls us to live in it. We show by our care of the environment that we respect God's detailed work of living art. *Tony Campolo*[14]

R E T R O - T O U R

Blessed are the merciful: for they shall obtain mercy. Blessed are the pure in heart: for they shall see God. Blessed are the peacemakers: for they shall be called the children of God.

And the doing of which Jesus speaks is a million miles from religious observance. This is not about how we conduct ourselves in church, but about how we live in the world he has given us. The merciful show mercy in every dimension of their lives – in every reaction and relationship. The pure in heart seek purity in every sense: they love innocence; they covet naiveté; they look to believe the best in every circumstance. Peacemakers look to make peace wherever it has been broken – in domestic situations; in local and global wars; in our bruised and battered environment. Every act that shows mercy; every act that seeks purity; every act that brings peace reflects, somehow, the character and nature of the Creator.

The hard-of-hearing Hebrew halfway down the mountain who thought he heard Jesus say 'Blessed are the cheese-makers' was not entirely wrong. The Kingdom is not only about what you are, it is also about what you make of what you are.

⊖ S U B W A Y M A P

STATION
Psalm 24:3-6 – an early invitation for those whose hearts are pure, and who hunger after God, to seek him.

CONNECTIONS
Hebrews 12:14-17 – an expansion of just what it means to be pure-hearted and seek peace.
James 2:12-13 – a statement of the triumph of mercy.

4. WHAT WILL THE NEIGHBOURS SAY?

Location *Matthew 5:10-12.* Blessed are those who are persecuted because of righteousness, for theirs is the kingdom of heaven. Blessed are you when people insult you, persecute you and falsely say all kinds of evil against you because of me. Rejoice and be glad, because great is your reward in heaven, for in the same way they persecuted the prophets who were before you.

Landmarks Even persecution can be a blessing from the hand of God; the prophetic call will always inspire opposition; it is in suffering that the strength to love is found.

What to see Only one of the Beatitudes needs repeating. Only one is amplified and qualified by Jesus. Why? Almost certainly because this is the most subversive statement of all, the most surprising in an already surprising discourse. It is hard enough to equate poverty with joy and to see hunger and thirst as desirable, but here Jesus is asking us to go one step further. He asks us to see persecution as a blessing from God. In his qualification of what this might mean, he includes insults and false accusations, and cites the experience of the prophets, whose sufferings included public ridicule and humiliation, imprisonment, death threats and violence. In the case of the last prophet – the cousin of Jesus, John the Baptist – persecution finally ended in murder. The 'they' who 'persecuted the prophets who were before you' includes both political and religious leaders and the ordinary members of the prophets' own families and communities. Jesus is warning his followers that opposition to their choices will come from both near and far – from the powerful and

from the population – and that it will be both expressed and acted upon. This is perhaps the clearest statement Jesus makes that the kingdom of God is no pleasure cruise.

In *The Prophetic Imagination*, Walter Brueggemann writes 'The task of prophetic ministry is to nurture, nourish and evoke a consciousness and perception alternative to the consciousness and perception of the dominant culture around us.'[15] This Jesus does, supremely, is these Beatitudes. But if this truth is going to subvert the status quo, if this kingdom really is upside-down, then it will not be peacefully received by all. When you turn the pile over, it is those at the top of it who will complain. Those whose pursuit of money, sex and power has made them winners in the existing order of things are hardly likely to welcome the voice of sanity and conscience Jesus brings. To align your life with the prophetic call, as Jesus does here, is to invite persecution.

But in what sense can this persecution truly be received as blessing? Not in the sense that it simply doesn't matter. Jesus is not here trivialising the realities of persecution. Having lost his friend and cousin to the oppressor's sword, he is a man who knows that the pain of persecution is deep pain. Jesus stands with – not apart from – all those who have suffered torture, degradation and loss in the cause of truth and justice. But as strong as the pain is, there is a blessing which is stronger still. As C.S. Lewis says at

What to do

■ Take some time to learn and understand the reality of persecution in our age. Make contact with one of the organisations that deals with the persecution of Christians – Open Doors, Release International, Jubilee Campaign and Christian Solidarity all offer information and resources – or look into the work of Amnesty International, which works on behalf of all those unjustly imprisoned, whatever their faith. Reflect on how you might stand closer to the victims of oppression, and ask yourself what you can learn from their experience.

■ Take time to pray for the persecuted, and for those who persecute them. Make this a regular element in the pattern of prayer you follow.

■ Get hold of a copy of *Jesus Freaks*, published by Eagle in the UK and by Word in America, to read the gripping stories of Christian martyrs throughout history. Visit the book's companion site at http://www.jesusfreaks.net or the Voice of the Martyrs site at http://www.persecution.com.

Places to stay

I suffer in the West more than I did in Communist lands. My suffering consists first of all in longing after the unspeakable beauties of the Underground Church, the Church that fulfils the old Latin saying, *nudisnudum Christi sequi* (naked, follow the naked Christ). ... I have found truly joyful Christians only in the Bible, in the Underground Church, and in prison. *Richard Wurmbrand*[16]

Somehow, in the midst of our tears, a gift is hidden. Somehow, in the midst of our mourning, the first steps of the dance take place. Somehow, the cries that well up from our losses belong to our song of gratitude. *Henri Nouwen*[17]

R E T R O - T O U R

Blessed are they which are persecuted for righteousness' sake: for theirs is the kingdom of heaven. Blessed are ye, when men shall revile you, and persecute you, and shall say all manner of evil against you falsely, for my sake. Rejoice, and be exceeding glad: for great is your reward in heaven: for so persecuted they the prophets which were before you.

the moment in which Aslan has been shaved, beaten and destroyed by the magic at work in the world: there is 'a deeper magic'. Among the strands that make up the unexpected depths of this blessing, three stand out:

■ Persecution is a blessing because it tells us we are on the side of justice. If the perpetrators of violence and oppression act against us, they only confirm that truth is with us. It is those of us who are not persecuted who would do well, before God, to ask why.

■ Persecution is a blessing because it purifies our own desires and motivations. If poverty of spirit and purity of heart are our goals, the opposition of others may be the greatest help we have to attain them. The real enemies of true faith are not the persecutors that wake us in the night, but the possessions and comfort that lull the soul to sleep.

■ Persecution is a blessing because it puts us into contact with the deepest wells of God's love. There is no love deeper than love in the face of violent hate. Like a grindstone sharpening steel; like a fire purifying gold, opposition and persecution serve to bring out the very best of faith. No one welcomes such suffering for themselves, and no one wishes it on those they love. But in the mysterious economy of the kingdom, it emerges as a pearl of great price. To stand in solidarity with those who suffer in this way is to stand at the side of Jesus.

5. TAKE THE TASTE TEST

Location *Matthew 5:13*. You are the salt of the earth. But if the salt loses its saltiness, how can it be made salty again? It is no longer good for anything, except to be thrown out and trampled by men.

Landmarks Salt and light as the 'centre of the centre' of Jesus' message; the call to serve God as stewards of his world; the impossible made possible as salt is restored in Christ.

What to see There is a sense in which the Beatitudes are not just the beginning of the Sermon on the Mount, but its heart and soul. In these short, enigmatic sayings, Jesus introduces the principles that he will dedicate the rest of his teaching career to explaining and unfolding. They are principles that we could spend the whole of history exploring, and still not fully grasp. 'When we cannot, by searching, find the bottom', writes Matthew Henry, 'we must sit down at the brink and adore the depth.'[18] Wrapped up somehow in these principles – in their obscurity as much as in their clarity – is the mystery of what it means, before God, to be human. These are not religious platitudes, they are the opinions of the Creator of the universe on the way the world works: and the way it doesn't but should.

In the same way, the two verses that immediately follow – the historic statements of the calling to be salt and light – capture in essence the purpose of humanity. If the Beatitudes are the centre of this sermon, these verses are the centre of the centre, setting out the very heart of the Creator's appeal to his creation. The world has not come into being by some cosmic accident, and nor is the place of men and women in it accidental. Rather, it is the finely crafted work of a great artist, and the caretakers to whom he has entrusted it – the stewards in whose keeping he has left his very inheritance – are the subjects of his love and confidence. The words of Genesis capture the first commissioning of humankind: 'Fill the earth and subdue it. Rule over the fish of the sea and the birds of the air and over every living creature.'[19] Women and men were to be God's image-bearers in the earth, ruling over it as he would rule: preserving the good, bringing out all the many flavours locked within it. You are the salt of the earth, Jesus says, you have a purpose. Every gift you have been given has been given to this end. Your intelligence and artistry; your creativity and character; your strength and stamina – these have been given to you so that you can work with God to unlock the full potential of his garden. Salt was not simply an add-on to first century life: it was essential to it, much as refrigeration has become indispensable to the twenty-first century home. The fact that salt beef survives to this day as a kosher delicacy speaks of the usefulness of salt as a preserver of food – and a guard against food poisoning.

To a Hebrew audience, salt also spoke of covenant. A 'covenant of salt' was seen in the ceremonial context as a binding or unbreakable agreement.[20] In many traditional cultures, the purifying, antiseptic and preserving qualities of salt have led to it being seen as symbolic of

---

What to do

■ Take a handful of salt. Rough-grained sea-salt is best, but the refined variety will do. Hold the salt in your hand as you reflect on its power: to preserve from rot, and to bring out the many flavours of food. Ask God to show you how your humanity can be made 'salty' in its role on the earth.

■ Reflect on the role that refrigeration plays in our more technological age. If your fridge and freezer failed or were taken away, how long would it be before you began to count the cost in food lost and ruined?

■ Re-read the accounts of the creation in Genesis 1 and 2, each culminating in the central role of women and men as stewards of God's garden world. Pray for a deeper understanding of this role, and of its implications in the urban landscapes of our age.

fidelity and friendship. To this day in Arab societies the sharing of salt is seen as central to the giving and receiving of hospitality. For those familiar with these things, the term 'salt of the earth' would come as a call to return to the God-given covenant role – in which the Jewish nation was seen as God's chosen representative for the world.

Places to stay

The core of Christian revelation is that Jesus Christ is the sole legitimate Lord of all human lives. *H Kraemer*[23]

There is not one square inch of the entire creation about which Jesus Christ does not cry out 'This is mine – this belongs to me.' *Abrham Kuyper*[24]

And if, in his love, he has wished to make men his collaborators in the work of salvation, the limit of their power is very small and clearly defined. It is the limit of the wire compared with the electric current. We are the wire, God is the current. Our only power is to let the current pass through us. *Carlo Carretto*[25]

R E T R O - T O U R

Ye are the salt of the earth: but if the salt have lost his savour, wherewith shall it be salted? it is thenceforth good for nothing, but to be cast out, and to be trodden under foot of men.

Either way, whether the background to these verses is the creation mandate of Genesis or the covenant role of Leviticus, they represent a clear call to return to the purposes of God: to live a life marked out not by accident and opportunity, but by calling and design. The message of Christ is a call to return to first purposes: to enter in, once again, to the intentions of the Creator for his creatures. There is no higher purpose for humanity than to serve God as his salt – his health-preserving, flavour-enhancing, image-bearing representatives – in the earth. The greatest tragedy of any human life is to miss out on this calling, and on the power and resources offered with it.

The kingdom announcement that Jesus has come to make is that there is a way back. The fall will not have the final word, and God's creation project will not be lost: there is a way for women and men, through Jesus, to return to their God-given role and purpose.

That this way is only possible in Christ is captured in the strange reference to salt that has 'lost its flavour'. It was an ancient rabbinical question to ask 'How can salt that has lost its flavour be made salty again?' The sense of the question was rhetorical, because it was known that it was impossible to revive salt that had lost its taste and preserving power. The substance commonly used as salt was a white powder which contained sodium chloride, but much else besides. The sodium chloride, as the most soluble component, would be the first element to be washed out, leaving a powder that 'looked like salt, and was doubtless still called salt, but neither tasted nor acted like salt. It was just road dust.'[21] When this happened, there was no power in earth or heaven that could put the saltiness back in the salt.

But as Jesus said elsewhere in reference to camels and the eye of a needle, 'what is impossible with men is possible with God.'[22] The miracle of the kingdom announcement is that even the most salt-less of people, the man or woman who has run so far from the purposes of God that the image of the Creator is all but invisible in them, can be restored. The saltiness of human life is a gift of the Maker, lost in the fall. Only in the redemptive work of Christ can it be restored. The call to follow Christ is the call to become fully human once more.

 SUBWAY MAP

STATION
Genesis 1:28-31 – when humans were first called to be salt to the earth.

CONNECTIONS
Romans 12:1-2 – the calling to inward transformation for outward impact.
Colossians 4:2-6 – making the salt count in every conversation.

6. STRIKE A LIGHT!

Location *Matthew 5:14-16*. You are the light of the world. A city on a hill cannot be hidden. Neither do people light a lamp and put it under a bowl. Instead they put it on its stand, and it gives light to everyone in the house. In the same way, let your light shine before men, that they may see your good deeds and praise your Father in heaven.

Landmarks Light as the warmth and flame of life; light against the terrors of the night; light for friends and light for strangers; our light reflecting God's greater light; the folly of humankind written across the face of the earth.

What to see If salt is essential to a healthy diet and lifestyle, light is the very essence of life. In a pre-electric age, there was a strong awareness of how great darkness could be. D A Carson describes a similar setting in Canada, where it is possible 'to go camping hundreds of miles away from any city or town. If it is a cloudy night, and there is no phosphorous in the area, the blackness is total. A hand held three inches from your face cannot be seen.'[26] This would be a common experience to Jesus' first century audience – and any who had travelled at night far from city life would have known the terror that darkness can bring. In such velvet night, the slightest flame is a welcome sign that light and life persist. Those who first heard these words would have known:

■ That light is fire and fire is light. In pre-electric culture – which covers all but the most recent years of our history, and is still the norm in many parts of the world – the only source of light is flame. Where there is light, there is warmth, and the light of a flame is a 'living' light. To bring light to the world is not only to illuminate it in some cold, practical way, but to be a source of warmth and life.

■ That the light of a single lamp is fragile. The standard household lamp was a simple clay reservoir of olive oil with a crude wick. Its light spread hardly further than the few feet immediately around it, and it was vulnerable to the slightest breeze or draught. To read or work by such a lamp would involve huddling close and concentrating hard. There were no arc lights in the Israel of Jesus' day. The light of God in the human heart may be a gentle, fragile light: the power of your single flame may be small. But in God, it

has significance. The smallest of lights is light all the same.

■ That the light of a city is visible for miles around. By contrast to the single, fragile lamp, the collective light of the city takes on strength and power. For weary travellers, it is a sign of hope seen from afar. On the darkest of nights, even a city lit by the flame of oil-lamps would throw its light into the sky. 'The light from the city is reflected off the clouds, and the night, once perfectly black, is no longer quite so desolate.'[27] Thus the fragile, gentle light of one flame becomes, when joined to others, a powerful and visible symbol. The single lamp gives light for friends, the city light for strangers.

■ That the greatest single source of light and warmth is the sun. The phrase 'light of the world' was not unknown in the ancient world, and referred often to the sun. Jesus' audience knew that when the sun shone, no other light was needed. No

---

What to do

■ Get yourself to a place of total darkness: either by travelling, as D.A. Carson suggests, far from the city, or by shutting yourself into an unlit room. Take time to explore the meaning of darkness, and imagine a world without light. Then light a single flame, and reflect on what it means, in Christ, that light has come.

■ The single oil-lamp, Jesus says, gives light 'to everyone in the house'. Make a list of those close to you – figuratively those 'of your household' – and ask yourself what it means for you to be a source of light for them.

God of light and life, bring to my heart the warm and welcome flame of your love. Create in me a fire to bring light to your world.

Places to stay

You and I are called to be persons after the manner of Jesus. Nothing else matters. Our goal is to become as Christ, to always have his image before our eyes. Soren Kierkegaard once described two types of Christians: those who imitate Jesus Christ, and those who are content to speak about him. *Brennan Manning*[28]

Nothing can be certified as 'Christian' except it derive from Jesus; and the Church cannot represent itself as the Church of Christ if it does not come from him. The Church, its credibility and efficiency in our society, stand or fall according to whether it is the location and memorial of Jesus... *Hans Kung*[29]

R E T R O - T O U R

Ye are the light of the world. A city that is set on an hill cannot be hid. Neither do men light a candle, and put it under a bushel, but on a candlestick; and it giveth light unto all that are in the house. Let your light so shine before men, that they may see your good works, and glorify your Father which is in heaven.

one would waste precious oil by lighting lamps in daylight hours. In the same way, there is an implication here that the source of all light is the Father. Those who

⊖ S U B W A Y   M A P

STATION
Exodus 13:20-22 – the presence of God to give light to the people of Israel.
Exodus 25:31-40 – the role of a lamp in ceremonial worship to represent the presence and holiness of God.
Psalm 119:105-112, 129-136 – the law of God as a source of light for life's journey.

CONNECTIONS
John 1:1-9 – Jesus as God's light for humanity.
Revelations 21:22-27 – the future promise of a city warmed by the light of God himself.

see our faltering, human light will not thank us for it but will 'praise your Father in heaven'. The true light is the light of God: he is the one who illuminates, warms and gives life. The most we can do is reflect his greater light. The best our lives can be a is a mirror and memorial of the true source: God our maker.

There is an intriguing sting in the tail of these words. Speaking of a city on a hill, Jesus does not say that it should not be hidden but that it cannot. As he speaks, Jesus creates for his hearers the image of a night-time cityscape, directing their attention to its prominence in the landscape. By suggesting that such a city cannot be hidden, he is warning that the collective works of humankind, for better or worse, will be broadcast to the world. If a city chooses to stand more for darkness than for light, it cannot be hidden. If it sets its heart on prosperity at the expense of justice, its scars will be visible to all. The collective aspirations of women and men are gathered together in cities, and written on their skylines as readably and clearly as a public confession. Astronauts report that the contours of the Great Wall of China are visible from outer space: but this is not the only human project that is written indelibly across the earth's face. The sins of an individual can be hidden under a bucket: but the collective folly of humankind is visible to all.

 Tourist information Panel

TIP 1 Local Language

Four languages were common in Palestine during the time of Jesus' ministry.

■ **Aramaic** was one of a large group of similar languages which were used around the Fertile Crescent – a naturally fertile corridor from Iran to Egypt. We know that Jesus spoke Aramaic – talitha koum (*Mark 5:41*) and ephphatha (*Mark 7:34*) are examples of Jesus using Aramaic. This isn't surprising. Aramaic would have been the language of the peasant farmers and day-labourers in Galilee – the very people Jesus spent most of his time with.

■ **Greek** was brought to the region by Alexander's invasions some three hundred years previously. Most of Palestine and Syria was Hellenistic – in other words the region had accepted the Greek language and culture as the norm. It is likely that Greek would have been the language of commerce as well as the lingua franca of the day – the language you could expect most people to speak. However, Greek was socially a step up from Aramaic. Jesus may have spoken Greek, but we have no proof of this.

■ **Hebrew** was the religious language of Judaism. It is part of the same language family as Aramaic and so people who spoke Aramaic would have no problem understanding Hebrew. Hebrew was used in the synagogue, temple and in the Hebrew Scriptures (what became the Christian Old Testament). Since Jesus spoke in the synagogue and read from Isaiah, he clearly knew Hebrew.

■ **Latin** was the language of the Roman army of occupation. It was commonly used in official documents, public inscriptions and on high prestige buildings. Since Latin was the language of the forces of occupation there is little evidence that it was used outside of official circles in Palestine. Note that this was one of the languages which was used on the title placed above the cross.

▶

► **The Language of the Sermon**

The Sermon on the Mount is written in Greek although some people have tried to find an Aramaic background to it. In the end we will probably never know, this side of heaven, what language Jesus delivered the address in. However, the language Matthew writes in is a universal language – a language of the common people, a language known throughout the Mediterranean region. The Sermon is intended then for the common people – not just for a group of religious professionals or for the intelligentsia. The Sermon, like Copeland's *Fanfare*, is for the Common Man.

TIP 2 Local People

Who listened to the Sermon?

The Sermon begins with a mention that the disciples joined Jesus and then he began talking to them. The setting seems to be clear. Jesus has recently called the disciples, or at least some of them since definite mention has been made of only Peter, Andrew, James and John. They have begun to go with him through Galilee, initially working in the synagogues but also healing among the people. These preaching and healing miracles, we are told, draw crowds of people from Galilee and also from various territories to the south

and east of Galilee. It is with the thought of these crowds following him that Matthew relates the story of the Sermon on the Mount.

But who is it addressed to?

The beginning of the Sermon says that the disciples came to Jesus and he began teaching them. However, the end of the Sermon says that 'when Jesus finished saying these things, the crowds were amazed at his teaching'. It seems that even if the teaching was for the disciples, the crowd were still happy to eavesdrop. Indeed, Jesus must have made sure they could hear as well. The Sermon is for a more general audience than the disciples themselves. The intended audience, then, is not a group of religious devotees, but a crowd of interested onlookers – people who have left their homes and jobs to spend time following Jesus around to see what he is up to. If the Sermon is addressed to all of these people, then so are the Beatitudes and the Lord's Prayer. God's blessing and the offer of a relationship with the Father are not just the privilege of the inner circle but are offered to the masses, to the locals, to the rabble.

DISTRICT 2: LEGAL
The Old Court Buildings
Matthew 5:17-48

Orientation and information

Imagine for a moment that area of some great city you know that has long been associated with the law. At its heart, the dark and forbidding columns of the courthouse, where generations of the innocent and guilty have alike faced the trauma of trial. Picture the steps on which the public and press have gathered, time after time, to congratulate the winners, to welcome the newly released or to protest at the conviction of the wrongly accused. Scattered around this hub are the smaller buildings of the lesser courts, and spreading out from them the avenues and alleyways of the legal professionals. Solicitors' offices and barristers' chambers, each door adorned with its newly polished brass plaque: and behind the smooth facades, the dingy, airless rooms of clerks and administrators, of secretaries and typing pools. In the streets, men and women uniformly wigged and robed rush from place to place, their black capes flapping in the wind, their hands clasped around piles of paper encircled with ribbon and sealed with wax. On the sides of some buildings are carved inscriptions

in ancient and indecipherable script: words that must have once held meaning, but are all Greek to you now.

This is a district where tradition matters as much as truth, where precedent is as powerful a force as prescribed law. Here every step and stage of legal process is wrapped in ritual and layered with language the street stopped using centuries ago. Here educated experts pride themselves on their detailed knowledge of the most obscure of statutes. Here the case histories of countless generations are kept and catalogued, to be pulled from the shelf and dusted down with every faint chance they might shed light on new dilemmas. Here it is not the principle of love, but the particular provisions of law that carry the day. The robes are black and white, but the reasoning is every shade of grey.

This is very much the kind of area that Jesus moves into when he dares to talk about the Jewish law. Centuries old, and wrapped in layer upon layer of tradition, the law had become like an endless pass-the-parcel game, where every wrapper removed revealed another underneath, and no one ever got to the prize inside. With their robes and rituals and their endless discussion of the pettiest of applications, the experts and teachers of the day had become the crowned kings of judgmentalism. Learning by rote the minutiae of the law, they failed to see the majesty of the love behind it. They weren't just rearranging the Titanic's deckchairs – they were arguing about the relative merits of the different striped fabrics and using magnifying glasses to check for imperfections in the wood-grain. And all the time their ship – the ancient faith they had been asked to love and lead – was sinking.

And ordinary people lived confused and afraid in the shadow of the law courts they despised: unmoved by the rituals, unreached by the cold, archaic language, uninspired in the harshness of it all. Until Jesus came, with a pot of paint and a bagful of brushes, and began to paint the old dark buildings bright again.

HIGHLIGHTS

- Medicine man
- Change your altitude and your attitude
- In the land of the blind
- High fidelity
- The cheek of it!
- New laws for old?

1. MEDICINE MAN

Location *Matthew 5:17-20*. Do not think that I have come to abolish the Law or the Prophets; I have not come to abolish them but to fulfil them. I tell you the truth, until heaven and earth disappear, not the smallest letter, not the least stroke of a pen, will by any means disappear from the Law until everything is accomplished. Anyone who breaks one of the least of these commandments and teaches others to do the same will be called least in the kingdom of heaven, but whoever practices and teaches these commands will be called great in the kingdom of heaven. For I tell you that unless your righteousness surpasses that of the Pharisees and the teachers of the law, you will certainly not enter the kingdom of heaven.

Landmarks the God who offers not containment, but healing; waiting for grace to grow, until the scaffolding of commandment can come down.

What to see If I begin this paragraph, 'Don't think I am here to do away with free market economics', you will know two things. Firstly you will know that I think that you might think that getting rid of free market economics is exactly what I'm trying to do. Secondly, you will know that I must have given an indication in some previous sentence that could be construed as having that intention. Jesus was faced with just such a situation. His kingdom announcement was of an age of grace and freedom, an age in which God would reach out to the lost, the last and the least, regardless of their levels of religious observance. But to make such an announcement was to call into question centuries of tradition and law. Such was his emphasis on freedom that some were bound see him as an abolitionist when it came to the law.

But Jesus has not come to kill the law – he has come to bring it to fulfilment. His announcement is of a grace so wide and deep that it doesn't need to fear the law: a grace big enough to swallow the law whole. His approach is not to do away with the law, but to get behind it and under its skin, to understand why God put it there in the first place. There is an outer shell to the law: a thousand-fold list of tasks of command and control to clog up our lives in red tape. But there is also an inner purpose: the desire to be holy, to walk in the ways of God; to bring shalom into our lives, our communities and our world. Jesus makes a distinction between these two: the one passing, the other unchanging. 'The law will stand until the end of the age', writes Dewi Hughes, 'but Jesus has become the key to its meaning. … What he does is to go behind the surface meaning of the command and show that it has to do with the attitudes and motivations of the heart.'[30]

The law is to the kingdom of God as scaffolding is to a new building. While the building is taking shape, while its floors and beams are coming into place, the scaffolding has a part to play. And until the new construction is strong enough to stand on its own, the scaffolding will still retain a role. So it is with the law, and so it is in each of our lives. Until grace has so grown in us, so tamed our appetites and impulses with the outrageous love of our generous God that we will what he wills and obey from a free heart of worship – until that moment, we still need law to tell us what to do. This is the righteousness that surpasses that of the Pharisees, the rightness of heart that no amount of legalistic effort can bring: grace-righteousness; righteousness born of relationship, righteousness that flows out from us where the living waters of God have welled up. Where this righteousness is established the scaffolding can come down. But until that day – in full or in part – it must stay.

'Pharisees were content with an external and formal obedience to the letter of the law', John Stott has written. 'Jesus teaches us that God's demands are far more radical than this.'[31] The problem with the Pharisaic approach is that it keeps the letter of the law but ignores the purpose of the law, to bring to book the appetites and impulses whose free rein can wreak havoc on our personalities, our homes, our communities and our world. What we need is something deeper, something stronger. We need a cure that can get to the very heart of the problem – to the centre of our being where selfishness lives and indulgence and cowardice hide. Only with such a cure can we afford to throw away

What to do

■ Find a building in your area that is being constructed or renovated with the help of scaffolding. Take a look at the relationship between the outer structure of the scaffold poles and the inner structure of the building. Consider your own life in these terms. To what extent has the building of grace grown within you, showing obedience to God with spontaneity and joy? To what extent do you still need the outer frame of commandment and control, the external discipline to complement your inner strength? In both cases, thank God for his provision – and pray for the more perfect healing, when the scaffolding can come down altogether.

■ Take a moment to reflect on the distinction between the outer form of the law: its petty, restrictive code of legalistic constraints – and the inner purpose; God's desire to set us free from the appetites and impulses that destroy us. Which is more present in your life? Is your Christianity a faith of liberation or legality? Are you petty and particular, or creative and carefree?

the law's crutch. It is such a cure that Jesus comes to offer. He knows, as he speaks these words, that the Father has already set the wheels in motion that will make this self-transforming righteousness possible. Only he knows how great is the grace that will at any moment be released.

What is true in the wider theological sense of the law is also true in the detail of the everyday, where it is often the word discipline rather than the word law with which we argue. In an anti-legalistic age, we are suspicious of the external disciplines that prop up our intentions and supplement the strength of our will where it is weak. But as a result we struggle with addictions and compulsions, and live lives distorted by desires we know we should control, but can't. Don't be afraid, Jesus is saying here, to admit to your need of

help. Don't be embarrassed if there is still scaffolding outside the building of your life. This is the now-but-not-yet of salvation. Grace may be won in an instant, but it takes a lifetime to reach the furthest corners of our appetites. The law has been God's medicine for a sick world: containing the sickness and controlling

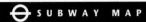 **SUBWAY MAP**

STATION
Psalm 119 (the long one). An extended meditation on the benefits and blessings of the law of God.

CONNECTIONS
Romans 7 and 8 – the condemnation that comes through the law, and the glorious liberation of Christ!

Places to stay

The word Christian means different things to different people. To one person it means a stiff, uptight, inflexible way of life, colourless and unbending. To another it means a risky, surprise-filled venture, lived tiptoe at the edge of expectation… But if we restrict ourselves to biblical evidence, only the second image can be supported: the image of the person living zestfully, exploring every experience – pain and joy, enigma and insight, fulfilment and frustration – as a dimension of human freedom, searching through each for sense and grace. *Eugene Peterson*[32]

Ultimately, faith is the only key to the universe. The final meaning of human existence, and the answers to the questions on which all our happiness depends cannot be found in any other way. *Thomas Merton*[33]

R E T R O - T O U R

Think not that I am come to destroy the law, or the prophets: I am not come to destroy, but to fulfil. For verily I say unto you, Till heaven and earth pass, one jot or one tittle shall in no wise pass from the law, till all be fulfilled. Whosoever therefore shall break one of these least commandments, and shall teach men so, he shall be called the least in the kingdom of heaven: but whosoever shall do and teach them, the same shall be called great in the kingdom of heaven. For I say unto you, That except your righteousness shall exceed the righteousness of the scribes and Pharisees, ye shall in no case enter into the kingdom of heaven.

the disease. But in Jesus, healing is promised – and when healing comes, the only place for pill-boxes is the dustbin. It is not the law that Jesus has come to destroy, but the need for it.

2. CHANGE YOU ALTITUDE AND YOUR ATTITUDE

Location *Matthew 5:21-26*. You have heard that it was said to the people long ago, 'Do not murder, and anyone who murders will be subject to judgement.'

But I tell you that anyone who is angry with his brother will be subject to judgement. Again, anyone who says to his brother, 'Raca,' is answerable to the Sanhedrin. But anyone who says, 'You fool!' will be in danger of the fire of hell. Therefore, if you are offering your gift at the altar and there remember that your brother has something against you, leave your gift there in front of the altar. First go and be reconciled to your brother; then come and offer your gift. Settle matters quickly with your adversary who is taking you to court. Do it while you are still with him on the way, or he may hand you over to the judge, and the judge may hand you over to the officer, and you may be thrown into prison. I tell you the truth, you will not get out until you have paid the last penny.

Landmarks The real issue is not murder, but anger; don't cut the weeds back, kill the root; get yourself down off the mountain!

What to see Jesus moves on from an overview of the purpose of the law to look more closely at its particular provisions. His starting place is murder. The first social sin recorded in the Book of Genesis[34], murder is the world's oldest crime. In one way or another, it is illegal in every known human culture. Though the theft of property runs a close second in the 'universal crime' stakes, murder, the theft of breath and life, heads the list. But murder, according to Jesus, is not the problem. Murder is not the disease, it is a symptom.

The Genesis account of Cain and Abel – a story which pre-dates the law but carries in itself the deepest sense of the horror of murder – provides a valuable back-drop to the words of Jesus given here. When Cain is eaten up with jealousy of his brother Abel, the question God puts to him is 'Why are you angry?' It is anger that festers in the soul of Cain and ultimately issues in violence and murder. Even then – back before the law was given – it was clear that the issue was anger, even if the outcome was murder.

It is here that Jesus points to the inadequacy of the law – its inability to bring us into true holiness. The law can deal with murder. Murder can be contained and controlled by legal prescript. But it cannot thus be healed. For healing, you must get to the heart of hate and anger, and here the law is impotent. It is as if the law is a doctor trained in diagnostics, but ignorant and incompetent in treatment. It can tell us what the problem is, but offers us no help to solve it.

Jesus uses characteristically strong language to get across the severity of the real problem. He is not suggesting that everyone who ever utters the word 'fool' is heading straight to Hell. Rather, he is using this dramatic image to make it clear that hatred is more serious than murder. The inner drive is more potent than the outer act. It is not murder that eats away at our humanity, destroying the image of God in us, but hatred. It is not murder that, unchecked, will rob us of our place in God's salvation plan, but anger. 'Look to the heart', Jesus is saying, 'get to the root of the problem'. All the law can do is cut the weeds back: stepping in with each new murder to administer justice. But until the root is dealt with, this can only ever be containment. Only grace, the free self-giving of Christ in our place, can kill the root.

As so often in the words of Jesus, after the 'but I tell you' comes a 'therefore'. Given that the root of anger is so strong, given

What to do

■ **Make a list**. Not of the people you would happily murder... but of all those against whom you have grievances, however trivial. It can be a mental list or, if you feel able, a written list. Include situations where no open conflict has yet erupted, but where you know in your heart that it could blow at any moment. Reflect on who these people are; on what the root of your anger is; and on what the words of Jesus mean in your situation.

■ **Make a date**. Select at least one of the people on your list and set a target date by which you will, at the very least, have made the first move towards ending or averting conflict.

■ **Make a step**. Take a step in the right direction, even if it is small. Send a card; make a call; plan to say hello next time you meet, instead of flashing the icy stare and grunting. If need be, find a go-between who knows and respects you both, and ask them what the first step might be.

■ **Make a change**. Commit yourself to the long-term healing of broken relationships, and the long-term avoidance of anger. Know your own danger-zones, and learn to avoid them. Commit yourself to peace.

that the real issue is not the actions that issue from dark hearts, but the darkness that is in them, given that the fires of Hell are fuelled by the attitudes we hide: given all this, Jesus says, take action! The example that follows appears trivial. After talk of murder, hell and judgement, it seems mundane to move to a simple dispute between neighbours. But that is entirely the point. If we are to strike at the root of anger, we must kill it young. The battle fought in the trivial issues will never need to be fought with real guns. Deal with the small grievances. Deal with anger when it surfaces in the everyday. Deal with road rage; with the sharp tongue;

with the neighbour you've stopped speaking to. Get these things settled before they grow into full-blown conflict. Recognise that grace, by striking at the root, leaves no house room for even the hint of hatred. How many of the wars that have killed millions down the years have been started by men who refused to deal with hatred when it was local and private? How many convicted murderers could have stayed on the right side of the law if only they had found a cure for anger?

A mountain climber who strays too high, too fast without oxygen will experience a strange array of illnesses. Dizziness may

Places to stay

If only there were evil people somewhere insidiously committing evil deeds, and it were necessary only to separate them from the rest of us and destroy them. But the line dividing good and evil cuts through the heart of every human being. And who is willing to destroy a piece of his own heart? *Aleksandr Solzhenitsyn*[35]

In our era the road to holiness necessarily passes through the world of action. *Dag Hammerskjold*[36]

R E T R O - T O U R

Ye have heard that it was said of them of old time, Thou shalt not kill; and whosoever shall kill shall be in danger of the judgement: But I say unto you, That whosoever is angry with his brother without a cause shall be in danger of the judgement: and whosoever shall say to his brother, Raca, shall be in danger of the council: but whosoever shall say, Thou fool, shall be in danger of hell fire. Therefore if thou bring thy gift to the altar, and there rememberest that thy brother hath ought against thee; Leave there thy gift before the altar, and go thy way; first be reconciled to thy brother, and then come and offer thy gift. Agree with thine adversary quickly, whiles thou art in the way with him; lest at any time the adversary deliver thee to the judge, and the judge deliver thee to the officer, and thou be cast into prison. Verily I say unto thee, Thou shalt by no means come out thence, till thou hast paid the uttermost farthing.

come, and vomiting. Blisters may appear on the skin, and sores. Vision may be affected, and hearing. But all of these are only symptoms, and dealing with one or all of them won't bring healing. The real problem is the altitude – and there is only one cure: get down off the mountain.

The law can only ever deal with symptoms: it takes grace to deal with the cause. If you want to stay clear of murder, Jesus says, deal with anger.

 **SUBWAY MAP**

STATION
Genesis 4:1-12 – the tragic tale of Cain and Abel

CONNECTIONS
Acts 9:1-31 – the dramatic conversion of a would-be murderer.

3. IN THE LAND OF THE BLIND

Location *Matthew 5:27-30*. You have heard that it was said, 'Do not commit adultery.' But I tell you that anyone who looks at a woman lustfully has already committed adultery with her in his heart. If your right eye causes you to sin, gouge it out and throw it away. It is better for you to lose one part of your body than for your whole body to be thrown into hell. And if your right hand causes you to sin, cut it off and throw it away. It is better for you to lose one part of your body than for your whole body to go into hell.

Landmarks Wandering hands or roaming eyes: whichever you are plagued by, take radical action to end your anatomical roving.

What to see There is a story told of Moses coming down from Mount Sinai to address the Hebrew people. As they rush forward to hear what God has decreed, Moses says, 'Friends, I have some good news and some bad news. The good news is – I've got him down from 45 to ten. The bad news is, adultery's still in.' Of all the commands of God, none have caused so much controversy and offence over the years as those to do with sexuality. Of all the rooms of the house, the bedroom is the last we invite God into. In the post-modern age, sexuality is seen as an arena of inviolable personal rights: I have a right to fulfilment and satisfaction, where and with whom I choose, and what I do with

my body, my thoughts and my DVD player is entirely my own affair.

Not so, says Jesus. Your sexuality, as much as any other aspect of your life, is up for healing and renewal in the coming kingdom of grace. And those things done and thought in secret – yes, even those things – must be dealt with. The model Jesus has established in dealing with murder – where the law handles the symptoms, but he names the cause – is here applied again. Adultery is not the problem, we are told, lust is. Look to the heart. Deal with the root of the issue.

Before exploring this further, it is important to note that Jesus deals with issues of personal lust in the context of adultery. The principle behind this is not to take a negative view of sex so much as a positive view of marriage. Because marriage is seen as a covenant – a relationship sealed in vows before the face of God – adultery is seen as covenant breaking. Unregulated sexual expression is avoided because it has relational and social implications. It is never 'just the two of us' – the family and wider community are in the bedroom with you! Jesus takes a strong line on adultery because he believes – popular or not – that marriage matters.

It would be easy to dismiss this concept of 'adultery in the heart' as prudish, petty and legalistic – if it wasn't for the fact that pornography is one of the planet's biggest businesses and women and children the

What to do

■ **Search your heart**. There is nothing to be gained from the deliberate generation of false guilt. But if there is a problem in your heart in this area, it needs to be brought into the light.

■ **Sweep your house**. There is nothing quite like a dustbin for storing pornography. Or if you're worried someone might find it, try the local dump. The council amenity sites of the world have an important ministry in this area.

■ **Seek out a friend**. More often than not, it is secrecy and silence that imprisons us. If there is someone you can trust, trust them. Ask them not only to hear you, but to help you. One proven strategy is to give them permission to ask you the questions no one else asks.

■ **Set the boundaries**. It may be that for you the adultery in question is not in your head but in your bed: you may be living already beyond the boundaries Jesus here recommends. If this is the case, take the time to reflect on the issues. Think, read and pray. Talk to those you trust. Consider not just the tightly summarised teaching Jesus gives here, but all the New Testament teaching on sexual matters. Consider whether the wisdom of a first century itinerant rabbi might not after all prove wise for the twenty-first century world.

world over are prisoners of various forms of sexual slavery. At every stage of human technological growth, the pornographers have been there to re-invent their industry, adapting first to print, then to film and now, supremely, to the internet. Call Jesus a killjoy if you will, but he was onto something here. C.S. Lewis writes, 'Suppose you came to a country where you could fill a theatre by simply bringing a covered plate onto the stage and then slowly lifting the cover so as to let everyone see, just before the lights went out, that it contained a mutton chop or a bit of bacon. Should you not think that in

that country, something had gone wrong with the appetite for food?'[37]

It would have been tempting, sitting on a breezy Palestinian hillside in daylight; the sun bouncing off the lake below, children running about at the feet of their parents, to avoid these issues altogether. The nine o'clock watershed had not been passed – this was family time. But Jesus is having none of it. 'I know, and you know', he is saying, 'how powerful these forces are. I know, and you know, what damage they can do.' Let's have no pretence that sex is all fun and no one gets hurt. Jesus is not –

Places to stay

Lust produces bad sex, because it denies relationship. Lust turns the other person into an object, a thing, a non-person. Jesus condemned lust because it cheapened sex, it made sex less than it was created to be. For Jesus, sex was too good, too high, too holy to be thrown away by cheap thoughts. *Richard Foster*[38]

The wise person doesn't know more, she or he lives more. All the truth is lived truth for the wise, truth tested and refined and tempered in the crucible of street and market, bedroom and kitchen, cancer and rejection, children and marriage. Wisdom is lived truth. *Eugene Peterson*[39]

R E T R O - T O U R

Ye have heard that it was said by them of old time, Thou shalt not commit adultery: But I say unto you, That whosoever looketh on a woman to lust after her hath committed adultery with her already in his heart. And if thy right eye offend thee, pluck it out, and cast it from thee: for it is profitable for thee that one of thy members should perish, and not that thy whole body should be cast into hell. And if thy right hand offend thee, cut it off, and cast it from thee: for it is profitable for thee that one of thy members should perish, and not that thy whole body should be cast into hell.

and never has been – anti-sex. There is no hint in the Bible – unless you misinterpret it through prudish eyes – of the up-tight, pallid fear of sex so often associated with the church. But neither is he blind to the real costs of rule-free sex. He is not neurotic, but neither is he naïve.

Once again, dramatic language is used to bring home the deep significance of these matters. Where we were threatened with Hell for saying 'fool', we are now told to dismember ourselves rather than tolerate lust. Once again, it is beyond foolish to take these words at face value. If every

man whose eye was ever lustful took this literally, none of us would get a driving licence. But the drama serves a purpose. It tells us:

■ **To take these things seriously**. Jesus is a man: he knows how often we will shrink away from dealing with these questions: keeping private what we do with our privates! If it takes shock tactics to get us out into the open, he will use them.

■ **To be self-aware**. Because there is a cloak of secrecy over all things sexual, it will often be the case that only we know what the issues are for us. Only you know if it is your eye that wanders, or your hand. Either way, it is time to stop ignoring it.

■ **To take radical action**. The gruesome images of eyeless heads and hand-less arms are not prescriptive but descriptive. They serve as a measure of the radical action that may be needed. If your weakness is stored on the hard-disk of your PC, wipe it clean or bin the computer. It is better to be without a computer at all than to be drawn into the living hell of uncontrolled indulgence.

Verse 28 makes it clear that Jesus sees himself as talking, here, to men. Rule-free sex is by no means an exclusively male domain: but it has been true historically that the abuse of sex is very often a male problem and that the victims, more often than not, are women and children. There is as much oppression of women in the

bedroom as in the boardroom, and the two are not entirely unconnected. Deal with it, men, Jesus is saying. Get your appetites under control, and stop treating the women in your lives as objects.

4. HIGH FIDELITY

Location *Matthew 5:31-37*. It has been said, 'Anyone who divorces his wife must give her a certificate of divorce.' But I tell you that anyone who divorces his wife, except for marital unfaithfulness, causes her to become an adulteress, and anyone who marries the divorced woman commits adultery. Again, you have heard that it was said to the people long ago, 'Do not break your oath, but keep the oaths you have made to the Lord.' But I tell you, Do not swear at all: either by heaven, for it is God's throne; or by the earth, for it is his footstool; or by Jerusalem, for it is the city of the Great King. And do not swear by your head, for you cannot make even one hair white or black. Simply let your 'Yes' be 'Yes,' and your 'No,' 'No'; anything beyond this comes from the evil one.

Landmarks Are you as good as your word? The issue is not divorce, but fidelity: can you be trusted to hold to the commitments you have made?

What to see You are in mid-flight, dozing through a magazine or film. A shudder shakes your seat and passes through your body. Halfway between waking and sleeping, your attention is

---

⊖ **S U B W A Y   M A P**

STATION 1
Samuel 11:1 – 12:10 – the tragedy of one man's inability to overcome lust, and the terrible consequences in his life.

CONNECTIONS
Psalm 51 – David's prayer of repentance and restoration.
I John 1:5 – 2:6 – the challenge to holiness comes with the promise of forgiveness.

caught by the 'ping' of the public address system, as the 'Seatbelts On' signs light up above your head. Moments later, the captain's soothing voice comes over the PA. 'Ladies and gentlemen, we are passing through some turbulence. Please return to your seats and fasten your safety belts.'

It is not within the remit of the Bible to issue such warnings in mid-passage – but if it were, there would surely be one here. If there is any aspect of the teaching of Jesus could be said to be turbulent, it is these words about divorce. 'This is partly because divorce is a complex and controversial subject', John Stott writes, 'but even more because it is a subject which touches people's emotions at a deep level.'[40]

Jesus is wading into a debate that was as hot in his day as it is in ours. Controversy was raging in the rabbinical community over the precise meaning of the law – and of Moses' interpretations of it. A longer exploration, recorded in Matthew 19:3-11, gives greater insight into Jesus' views on these complex issues, which revolved then as now around detailed questions both of divorce and of remarriage. These questions are complicated, intricate and fragile. They draw in not just the 'main players' of the marriage(s) in question, but a whole supporting cast of children, family members and the wider community. They carry very often a kind of pain that is deeply personal and keenly felt, and over which no one – religious leader or otherwise – has the right to trample.

No resolution can be brought to these questions in the space of a few words, and every case must be looked at by its own light, but there are three principles here which help to set parameters to our thoughts:

Firstly, Jesus is not replacing the old law with a new one. The kingdom announcement is about grace and healing, about giving us the power to live blessed human lives. It as foolish for Christians to build detailed legislation from these words as it was for the Pharisees to do the same to Moses.

Secondly, the real issue Jesus highlights is fidelity. Divorce is the symptom, but faithfulness is the goal. What will it take, he is asking, for men and women to be true to their promises? What kind of kingdom do we need to empower that level of trust? Stop arguing over pedantic interpretations of divorce law: start working towards a culture of fidelity.

Thirdly, Jesus is the Messiah of the second chance. Whatever scalpel he brings to issues of divorce and adultery – as to issues of murder, hatred, theft and revenge – he does so in the wider context of healing. There is no action so vile that it cannot be forgiven. There is no life beyond the reach of his redemption. Just when you feel cornered by the dead-end of an uncompromising view of divorce, the trap door of redemptive grace springs open.

I was devastated when my parents' marriage fell apart. Emotionally, financially,

What to do

■ Pray for those whose marriages are passing through turbulent times. Pray that healing will have greater strength than hurt.

■ Pray that in your own life – in every relationship you put your hand to – you will know the meaning of fidelity.

■ Pray for the gift of simple truth – that you would be able to say what you mean, and mean what you say, and be known as someone 'true to their word'.

Father, for all those whose family journey is taking them through rocky times – may your overwhelming grace bring peace and healing. For all those for whom the break-up is in the past, who live now with the fall-out and the memory – may your overwhelming grace bring peace and healing. For all of us, as we deal daily with one another's weaknesses and failings – may your overwhelming grace bring peace and healing.

Places to stay

Fidelity is the ethical element which enhances natural love. *Emil Brunner*[41]

Live together in forgiveness. Don't insist on your rights. Don't blame each other, don't judge or condemn each other, don't find fault with each other, but accept each other as you are, and forgive each other every day from the bottom of your hearts. *Dietrich Bonhoeffer on married life*[42]

R E T R O - T O U R

It hath been said, Whosoever shall put away his wife, let him give her a writing of divorcement: But I say unto you, That whosoever shall put away his wife, saving for the cause of fornication, causeth her to commit adultery: and whosoever shall marry her that is divorced committeth adultery. Again, ye have heard that it hath been said by them of old time, Thou shalt not forswear thyself, but shalt perform unto the Lord thine oaths: But I say unto you, Swear not at all; neither by heaven; for it is God's throne: Nor by the earth; for it is his footstool: neither by Jerusalem; for it is the city of the great King. Neither shalt thou swear by thy head, because thou canst not make one hair white or black. But let your communication be, Yea, yea; Nay, nay: for whatsoever is more than these cometh of evil.

socially; my father's decision to leave my mother for a woman twenty years his junior brought havoc to our lives. To the very moment of her death 25 years later, my mother never entirely recovered from the break-up. I was ten years old, and the years of my adolescence were over-shadowed more than anything by the absence of my father. I will never underestimate the chaos that divorce can cause. But neither will I put it beyond healing. I have experienced grace beyond measure in the intervening years. My own marriage has been a source of healing. My children are a gift of inestimable worth. The ground that was scorched by the napalm-fire of rejection and abandonment has been replanted, and grows now with the rich greenery of grace. Jesus may take a strong stance on divorce: but he reserves his greater strength for recovery and healing.

It is instructive that the treatment of divorce flows directly into consideration of oaths and vows. The issues are closely linked in our day because marriage is one of the few contracts that we continue to express in terms of public vows. In the Jewish community this was not the case – there were hundreds of occasions for the swearing of oaths. Like an incorrigible borrower ['This time I really, really, really promise I'll pay you back next week…'], the oath-taker would use increasingly extravagant vows as a smoke-screen for the absence of self-discipline. Into this mayhem Jesus speaks a simple word – let your 'yes' be 'yes'. As fidelity is the real

issue in divorce, so honesty is the real issue here. If you mean what you say, it's unnecessary to swear it – and if you don't mean what you say it's blasphemy. Get the 'expletive deleted' out of your grammar, and state the simple truth. Be as good as your word.

5. THE CHEEK OF IT!

Location Matthew 5:38-42. You have heard that it was said, 'Eye for eye, and tooth for tooth.' But I tell you, do not resist an evil person. If someone strikes you on the right cheek, turn to him the other also. And if someone wants to sue you and take your tunic, let him have your cloak as well. If someone forces you to go one mile, go with him two miles. Give to the one who asks you, and do not turn away from the one who wants to borrow from you.

Landmarks The fine art of cheek turning: a new form of karate, or an even more radical way to resist, absorb and transform the power of hatred?

What to see Ex-gangster Ken Lancaster tells an insightful story about the impact of this text. Having for a long time been associated with the likes of the Kray brothers, and known throughout London as a hard man, he was dramatically converted in his prison cell one Christmas Eve. Not long after, when he had served his sentence, the rumour began to circulate that the former boxer had found religion and 'gone soft'. Those with grievances against him saw their opportunity. He was leaving a pub one night when an old rival stopped him and punched him on the jaw. A tense silence followed as the assailant waited to see if this new Christian would turn the other cheek. Ken, not long converted, had a choice to make. He knew the Bible called him to do just that.

'And so I did' he says, 'I turned my face and let him hit me again. And then I beat him to a pulp.'

Ken uses the story to illustrate the truth that sanctification takes time – the sinner does not become the saint in a day's turning. But it also illustrates the extent to which the ideas of Jesus have entered the linguistic gene pool of our culture. We are intrigued and fascinated, amused and puzzled by this radical idea. Of all the possible responses to a slap on the face, asking for another is the most unnatural. So what is Jesus saying to us here? There is more than one surprise in these words.

■ The first surprise is that this is not a call for weakness, but for strength. It is the weak person who, when hit, immediately hits back. It is through weakness that violence begets violence and escalates out of all control. Even the admonition to take 'an eye for an eye', drawn from the Old Testament[43] is in part a compensation for human weakness. Knowing how easily the offended will rush to inflict 'punitive damages'; this law limits them to, at most,

reciprocal revenge. It take[s] keep within these bounds – bu[t] for even more. What strength doe[s] to kill the violent instinct altogether a[nd] keep peace?

■ The second surprise is that these words describe activity, not passivity. It is a choice to turn the other cheek, an action. We make that action not as passive victims, but as active lovers. Violence cannot cure violence any more than pus can cure infection. Only the antidote to violence can heal it – and the antidote is an act of love.

■ The third surprise about this way of reacting.... is that it works. To respond to violence with violence might settle a score. It might teach your assailant a lesson. It might, for an instant, make you feel better. But the response of peace can do something more: something the best-aimed punch in the world cannot aspire to. It can change the person on the giving end of violence. At the height of the Civil Rights protests in 1960s America, when the black population were the victims of unthinkable mistreatment, Martin Luther King wrote: 'To our most bitter opponents we say: "We shall match your capacity to inflict suffering by our capacity to endure suffering. We shall meet your physical force with soul force... Throw us in jail, and we shall still love you. Send y[our] hooded perpetrators of violenc[e] community at the mid[…] beat us and leave[…] shall still love you. B[…]

ur capacity to
freedom, but
hall so appeal
e that we shall
d our victory

This is not any easy road, and it is not painless. King was one of those who learnt this to his cost, and paid the bill with his life. But he was also proved right in the end, as the power of resistant love tore into the strongholds of racism in America. This is the power Gandhi, the great icon of peaceful resistance, called 'truth-force'[45], the power that comes from knowing right and justice to be with you. That Jesus understood the cost of the

choices he was asking for, and their political implications, is clear from the illustrations he continues with. In particular, the image of being 'forced to go one mile' almost certainly refers to the right of the Roman occupying army to commandeer at random any Jewish citizen, forcing them to carry his bags for one mile. The hatred of the Jews for their oppressors – as violent and unjust as we know the Nazi occupations of the Second World War to have been – was fed by these repeated, daily humiliations. They were symbolic not of personal violence but of institutional injustice. They reminded the Jewish citizen of his powerlessness at the hands of an occupying army. They were racist and

---

What to do

■ Know your enemy. For the Jews, it was the Roman occupier who oppressed. Who is it for you? Who has power over you, and uses it unjustly? And what might it mean for you to practise resistant love?

■ Know your heart. What are the places in your heart where the will to violence hides? In what circumstances do you find yourself not turning the left cheek so much as putting in the right boot? Offer these places up to God, and invite him to give you the temper of Jesus.

■ Know your strength. Who are the victims of oppression in your world? Who are those facing, even now, the challenge to turn the other cheek? Might it be that you have strength to offer such people – that the difficult decision they make to choose resistant love could be made easier by your solidarity, your letters, your prayers?

DISTRICT 2: LEGAL

Places to stay

Even in conditions of profound injustice, even in servitude and discord, Christian faith enables men not to despair of peace, liberty and justice. It allows hope to penetrate even where there is nothing left to hope for; a love to persist that includes even one's enemy; and work to be done for the humanisation of man and society, even where men are busy spreading inhumanity. *Hans Kung[46]*

You only have power over a people so long as you don't take everything away from them. But when you've robbed a man of everything he's no longer in your power – he's free again. *Aleksandr Solzhenitsyn[47]*

R E T R O - T O U R

Ye have heard that it hath been said, An eye for an eye, and a tooth for a tooth: But I say unto you, That ye resist not evil: but whosoever shall smite thee on thy right cheek, turn to him the other also. And if any man will sue thee at the law, and take away thy coat, let him have thy cloak also. And whosoever shall compel thee to go a mile, go with him twain. Give to him that asketh thee, and from him that would borrow of thee turn not thou away.

abusive laws, and fuel to the fire of the Zealots who called for violent resistance. But even here, Jesus says, you have a power stronger than revenge. Even here, where all hope is lost, and the light of freedom all but extinguished, there is strength in the force of resistant love.

Jesus was no more naïve about politics than he was about human sexuality. He knew what power was, and pain. He knew that the road of resistant love was a hard road to take. But he also knew it was the road to life.

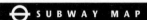

SUBWAY MAP

STATION
Leviticus 19:18 – an ancient command against revenge.

CONNECTIONS
Luke 23:26-43 – forgiveness at the very point of death.
Acts 7:54 – 8:1 – an act of grace that begins the journey into faith of a confirmed enemy.

6. NEW LAWS FOR OLD?

Location *Matthew 5:43-48.* You have heard that it was said, 'Love your neighbour and hate your enemy.' But I tell you: Love your enemies and pray for those who persecute you, that you may be sons of your Father in heaven. He causes his sun to rise on the evil and the good, and sends rain on the righteous and the unrighteous. If you love those who love you, what reward will you get? Are not even the tax collectors doing that? And if you greet only your brothers, what are you doing more than others? Do not even pagans do that? Be perfect, therefore, as your heavenly Father is perfect.

Landmarks Loving the alien: a power that overcomes the selfish gene. The call to perfection and the outrageous power of grace.

What to see Jesus provides three reasons for us to aspire to this love, which we make available to friend and enemy alike. Firstly, we love those who don't love us because they, like us, are the children of God. They may not wear our team colours, but underneath the strip they share our flesh. The God 'who makes his sun to shine' on each of us, is our Creator – and theirs. As such, every human bears his image, and is worthy of his dignity, no matter how far they have fallen. 'We are all in the gutter', Oscar Wilde wrote, 'Some of us are looking at the stars.' Many Christians have failed to understand this truth that God is the father of all humanity: so much do they want to claim him as 'their' God. But he is the one in whom 'we live and move and have our being'. We are all his offspring. No matter how little interest your enemies show in

God – there is no end to the interest he shows in them. Not one creature can draw breath without the patient love and mercy of God. He is, in this sense, the God of every person on the planet, no matter what faith they adhere to or if they resist faith altogether. He is Father to every Buddhist, every pagan, every atheist in the world. We love because God loves. We love because we are family. We love – as God does – even when no love is offered in return. We are used to talking of our global Christian 'family', but there is brotherhood and sisterhood also, in the God-made human family.

Secondly we love because only love can make a difference. Gordon Bailey's poem *The Idolator* captures the essence of the love that is no love at all.

'I love you,' he said, as he hugged her
'I love you', he said between sighs;
But she knew he adored his own image
as he looked at himself in her eyes.'[48]

If we love only those who love us, we are really only loving ourselves. What can such self-adoration do to change the world? What radical, life-transforming power is there in such ordinary and predictable affection? There is none. Such love will not end wars: it starts them. Such love will not wipe out poverty: it causes it. The love that will change us – and change our world – is the love the breaks the bars of self-love's prison, that takes us out of and beyond our small affections. Love of the familiar is easy. It is love of the other that has power.

Thirdly, we love unconditionally because we strive for the perfection of God. This strange phrase 'be perfect therefore..' ends this section of the Sermon and leaves us more desperate than ever. If we thought the approach to anger was tough, if we found lust and divorce hard to deal with, what are we to do with a challenge to match the perfection of God? Some have used this question as an excuse to devalue the whole Sermon. Since Jesus cannot possibly mean us to be perfect, this must be some literary device. The sermon is an interim ethic, or an impossible ideal. It is there just to show us how rotten we are, to send us rushing to the Mercy Seat. But these theories, clever as they are, just don't hold up. They cast Jesus as a devious and manipulative communicator, almost a trickster. Does this square with what we know of Christ?

Philip Yancey's resolution of this great dilemma, in *The Jesus I Never Knew*,[49] comes through holding in tension two aspects of the ministry of Jesus. On the one hand, 'he never lowered God's ideal'. The purposes of the Creator – that we should walk with him, live like him, and reflect his image in the earth – have never changed, no matter how far short of his ideal we fall. But on the other hand, Jesus lived and taught 'absolute grace'. He forgave, healed, restored, affirmed. He saw his Father in the worst of humanity, and always looked for the best. 'Grace is absolute, inflexible, all-encompassing. It extends even to the people who nailed Jesus to the cross: "Father forgive..."'[50]

What to do

There is little that we can do in the face of such overwhelming grace. But we can pray, knowing that without the strength of God we cannot even begin this journey into grace.

The Furnace of God's Love

Lord, I am poured out,
I come to you for renewal.

Lord, I am weary,
I come to you for refreshment.

Lord, I am worn,
I come to you for restoration.

Lord, I am lost,
I come to you for guidance.

Lord, I am troubled,
I come to you for peace.

Lord, I am lonely,
I come to you for love.

Come, Lord,
Come revive me
Come reshape me
Come mould me in your image.

Recast me in the furnace of your love.

David Adam[51]

DISTRICT 2: LEGAL

Places to stay

My telephone, I am told, links me with the world. So does my humanity. If only I employed my humanity as often as I use my telephone. *Gordon Bailey*[52]

Thunderously, inarguably, the Sermon on the Mount proves that before God, we all stand on level ground: murderers and temper-throwers, adulterers and lusters, thieves and coveters. We are all desperate, and that is in fact the only state appropriate to a human being who wants to know God. Having fallen from the absolute ideal, we have nowhere to land but in the safety net of absolute grace. *Philip Yancey*[53]

RETRO-TOUR

Ye have heard that it hath been said, Thou shalt love thy neighbour, and hate thine enemy. But I say unto you, Love your enemies, bless them that curse you, do good to them that hate you, and pray for them which despitefully use you, and persecute you; That ye may be the children of your Father which is in heaven: for he maketh his sun to rise on the evil and on the good, and sendeth rain on the just and on the unjust. For if ye love them which love you, what reward have ye? do not even the publicans the same? And if ye salute your brethren only, what do ye more than others? do not even the publicans so? Be ye therefore perfect, even as your Father which is in heaven is perfect.

Absolute ideals and absolute grace: this is the dual message of the Sermon on the Mount. The kingdom announcement is twofold. It is the affirmation that the purposes of God, and the standards of God, still stand. And it is the declaration – and this is new – that grace has been released. Grace enough to heal the very root of the appetites that the law could only ever contain. Grace enough to forgive you for your failure to be perfect yesterday and for your failure to be perfect today: and to go on forgiving every time you fail to be perfect. Grace that will slowly but surely begin to change you, until you find yourself reflecting more of God. Grace that is not medicine, but healing. Before such grace we are all naked: all we can do is receive. There is a cost, but it is not ours to pay.

Tourist information Panel

TIP 3 – Local Colour

Beatitudes

Beatitudes were actually very common in Jewish and Greek worship. Technically called a macarism, they can be found in many psalms – see Psalm 1.1 for a good example. Their usual form in Greek religion and popular myth was: blessed are the rich, the healthy, those with a good family to support them. In a society without government funded welfare support this was common sense – God was evidently smiling on you if everything was going OK.

On the other hand, Greeks and Romans were aware of the limits of human happiness: 'Blessed are the rich but death is evil.' Life is easier, and so you are more blessed, if you're rich. Death is a destruction of this happiness because it gets in the way of enjoying your wealth!

What is startling about the Beatitudes in this sermon is that Jesus reverses this trend. Rather than focusing on wealth and blessing and prosperity, these Beatitudes focus on poverty, mortality, humility, justice, mercy, purity, peacemaking and persecution – not the most obvious signs of the good life. For Jesus, living God's way is living counter to popular society.

Salt

Salt was of crucial importance in ancient societies. It was used for preservation, seasoning, purification and medicine, it was even used in sacrifices. The main source was rock salt or evaporated sea water rather than a pure substance manufactured by a chemical process. This impure salt could lose its saltiness and so would simply be a collection of impurities – suitable only for throwing on the path as a toxic weedkiller. Salt, of course, is only of use if it is used. It is when salt comes together with something else and reacts that it has an impact.

Lamps and Light

Of course there was no electricity in the ancient world. Most artificial light would come from either candles or oil lamps. Many of these lamps have been found in Greek and Roman remains all over the Mediterranean. So in most Galilean homes, a lamp was a fragile clay pot with a lip. Oil was put in the pot and a wick laid on the lip and lit. This pot was then placed on a stand to light the whole room. It was not a 100W bulb up on the ceiling. It probably gave out a little light although as Jesus says, it could light the whole household. In fact, such lamps were quite dangerous in a house where the floor was probably covered in dried grasses. The lamp was both a useful tool but also a potential disaster which could bring the whole house to ruin – or turn the world upside down.

TIP 4 – Local Headlines

The City on a Hill

Jesus suggests that you can't hide a city on a hill. It is quite likely that he was referring here to Sepphoris, the old capital of Galilee. Sepphoris is only now being excavated but in Jesus' time it was a growing city, being rebuilt by Herod Antipas as one of the capitals of his province. Eventually the city had a theatre, ten synagogues, several churches, a council chamber, an archive, two market places, temples, a city wall, a mint (Sepphoris minted its own coins), an extensive aqueduct system, and a cemetery, although much of this was built in the second and third centuries. Sepphoris was renowned for its citadel – built in pale stone at the top of a cliff. When the sun shone on the fortified stonework, it would have been difficult indeed to miss this symbol of military supremacy. As the chosen residence of many of the wealthy landowners of Galilee, Sepphoris was also a symbol of oppression, decadence and persecution.

Divorce

Two different schools of opinion seem to have been fighting over divorce during the first part of the century. The school of Shammai taught that a man had to divorce an unfaithful wife and that this was the only grounds for a divorce. The school of Hillel, on the other hand, taught that a man could divorce his wife for any reason. For both schools, the fault for divorce by a man is found in the woman, taking their cue from Deuteronomy 24:1. Clearly, by making an exception for sexual immorality, not necessarily on the part of the wife, rather than just adultery, Jesus broadened the focus. In Jesus' view, the fault could lie with either partner or with the marriage itself. It is clear from other references in the New Testament that divorce was not an accepted practice in the early church and where it did happen, it was seen as a sign of human frailty rather than normal practice.

DISTRICT 3: SPIRITUAL
A River Runs Through It

Matthew 6:1-18

Orientation and information

There is one feature that is common to most of the great cities of the world. More often than not they are built on rivers. For the most part, great cities are not to be found at the river's early stage, where it bubbles and splashes from the rocks: but in its later life, where its flow has become lazy, wide and strong. The river will often appear as a static object – a dark corridor criss-crossed with bridges – but in reality it never stops moving. Huge quantities of water pass through the city each day, bringing with it fish, life, debris and a steady flow of river traffic. Many motorists who think the only significant way into a city is by road would be amazed at the goods and services that are carried in afloat: and by what is carried out. It is the rivers of the world, more than any other feature, that serve to take away unwanted waste and sewage. Like blood through the heart, the river's constant flow is an invisible life in the depths of the city.

Rivers are also, for many people, places of peace and retreat. Not just for those who take out a boat to get away from the city's cars and clatter, but also for those who fish, or who choose to take a riverside walk. Lovers, in an evening, will be drawn to stroll along the water's edge: sensing the presence of a something deeper and more permanent than the city's fading lights. Children will come to play at the riverside. In many cities, parks and gardens will be so arranged as to run alongside the river, putting the peaceful flow of the water at the very centre of their oasis.

In the same way that we sense eternity when standing on the seashore, so the presence of the river in the city has spiritual power. The riverside gardens are a place of peace and repair; a place where you can set aside the pressures of city life and take stock. The air is a little cleaner here and the noise less. Nature has been given more freedom, the asphalt held back a little. Just to stand at the water's edge – at morning when the sun is just breaking and the city just waking; at evening when the river's flow is painted with the dancing reflections of a thousand lights – is to touch something of the beyond.

This is a valuable picture of the approach that Jesus takes to spirituality. The spiritual side of our lives, that aspect in which we pray, worship and devote ourselves to God, is not some separate area, distinct and cut off from the rest. It is more like a river that runs through the very centre of our lives. The presence of God is not to be sought in special religious activities but in the cut-and-thrust of the everyday. But it is to be sought. It takes a decision of the will, and effort of the mind and body, to cultivate spirituality. Just as it is possible to live and work in the city without once taking the time to walk through the riverside gardens, so it is possible to be so preoccupied in our lives – so taken up with activity – that we never stop to drink in the presence of God.

Jesus speaks to both the extremes that dog the spiritual quest, the extremes of religion and of un-religion. To both, he brings an alternative. A spirituality that is not about costumes and performance, but about life. A God who is not present in special buildings at set times, but who meets us in our own front room. A river of peace that runs through the very bustle of our lives – always there, always available to us. God is never more than a whisper away from us – 'the beyond in the midst of our lives'[54]. But he is a God who calls us apart. He invites us, moment by moment, to take the time to meet him. This is the paradox at the heart of Christian spirituality – it is a call for us to meet God in the everyday, and yet a call to step aside from the everyday to meet with God. The river may run through the heart of the city, but it still takes an effort to walk to it.

1. INTO YOUR ALMS AGAIN...

Location *Matthew 6:1-4.* Be careful not to do your 'acts of righteousness' before men, to be seen by them. If you do, you will have no reward from your Father in heaven. So when you give to the needy, do not announce it with trumpets, as the hypocrites do in the synagogues and on the streets, to be honoured by men. I tell you the truth, they have received their reward in full. But when you give to the needy, do not let your left hand know what your right hand is doing, so that your giving may be in secret. Then your Father, who sees what is done in secret, will reward you.

Landmarks Giving as the Secret Service of true holiness. Acts of love that come to God marked 'For your eyes only'. Contrasting heaven's smile with earth's applause.

HIGHLIGHTS

- Into your alms again
- Just deserts
- Yourkingdom.com
- Our daily breath
- Mapping the minefield
- Physical graffiti

What to see Jesus has set out his stall in describing the blessing of God – who gets wet when the water-pistol is fired, and he has poured out his understanding of the law – that God longs to give us healing, not containment. Now he turns to what might be described as the heartland of Jewish life: religious observance and practice. The three 'big issues' he tackles are giving to the needy, prayer and fasting. These are the three fruits that, to the Jewish mind, made up the basket of religion. Faith was not only about these matters: it spoke, as did the law, to the whole of life. But there was a sense that these three practices were central to pleasing God. Just as 'churchgoing' has become the accepted public mark of faith in our age so, to the Jews, these three activities marked out piety. And it went further than that. Because these three activities were seen as the trinity of piety, because they were seen as signs of holiness, it was their public expression that became important. Like householders competing to have the best display of Christmas lights, people would vie for the most pious public image. Their performance was polished and their religiosity rehearsed. Theirs was an Oscar-winning faith.

Jesus sets himself the delicate task of bursting this over-religious bubble without losing, in the process, the real need for spiritual discipline. He knows that it will not be possible to explore the holistic, humble, anti-legalistic spirituality he is about to propose without

challenging the performers on the block. So he makes no effort to hide his contempt. Three times he caricatures the hypocrites of the synagogues and streets. Three times he pours scorn on their performance. And three times he offers an alternative approach to the godly life. The answer to overblown religion is not to abandon the spiritual life altogether, but to take a deeper, less travelled road.

In this first picture, that of giving alms to the poor, Jesus introduces the three themes by which that deeper road is defined.

He establishes that piety is personal, not public.

It was never intended, Jesus argues, that acts of piety should be public. They are, rather, about the inner life, the secret garden of God in our lives. Unless this garden is growing, all the public piety on earth will ring hollow. True religion is about 'who you are when no-one's looking.' The arena in which we should seek and explore spiritual depth is not the public arena of the streets and temple, but the private arena of the heart and home.

He contrasts earth's applause with heaven's favour.

Those for whom the highest religious experience is an Oscar acceptance speech will find exactly what they are looking for. What they will not find is the blessing of God. When the applause has died down, and the gasps of the adoring fans are gone, they will realise, alone and bankrupt, that they have nothing. There is a reward for the spiritual searcher, but it is not found in the immediate gratification of impressing others. Worship can be played to the gallery or pleasing to God, but it will rarely be both. To seek God's light is to walk away from the limelight.

He puts the Father at the heart of the equation.

It is your Father who meets with you in the secret place. This is not the distant God who must be impressed with the orchestration of your worship and wooed with offerings of set-piece praise. God is not far from you, so that you have to throw your praise at him like bread to ducks. He is close to you, as close as breathing. He longs for intimacy, honesty, for heart to heart union. The orchestra will only get in the way. Don't make religion a substitute for relationship. One moment in the Father's presence is worth a thousand years of forced pretence.

The phrase Jesus uses – 'don't let your right hand know what your left hand is doing' – is the first rule of successful musicianship. It is when the hands act independently that harmony and beauty emerge. Pianists know that the right hand must do its job on the high notes even as the left hand, undisturbed, gets on with its role in the bass. So our giving to the poor should be so woven into the fabric of

What to do

■ Reflect on your own approach to alms-giving. Where does it sit on the spectrum that runs from public performance to private practice? Could you be doing more to invest in your 'hidden life with God'?

■ Think through the past seven days of your life. When have you had opportunities to give secretly? Did you take the opportunity, or let it slip by?

■ Make a plan to become a 'secret giver'. Decide on a level at which you want to give – whether it is money, time or some other form of help. Then ask God to show you the when and where of giving: in situations only he knows about.

Teach me, O God, to give to others as freely as you have given to me.

Save me, O God, from the temptation to use giving as a public performance, designed to impress all who see it.

Show me, O God, those to whom it is my privilege, in your plan, to give.

Places to stay

I saw a stranger yestereen. I put food in the eating place, drink in the drinking place, music in the listening place, and in the sacred name of the Triune, He blessed myself and my house, my cattle and my dear ones. And the lark said in her song, often, often, often goes the Christ in the stranger's guise. *The Book of Cerne*[55]

The man who has no inner life is the slave to his surroundings. *Henri Frederic Amiel*[56]

R E T R O - T O U R

Take heed that ye do not your alms before men, to be seen of them: otherwise ye have no reward of your Father which is in heaven. Therefore when thou doest thine alms, do not sound a trumpet before thee, as the hypocrites do in the synagogues and in the streets, that they may have glory of men. Verily I say unto you, They have their reward. But when thou doest alms, let not thy left hand know what thy right hand doeth: That thine alms may be in secret: and thy Father which seeth in secret himself shall reward thee openly.

our lives that our other activities are not even interrupted for the act. Only then can you launch yourself on waves of music. Only then will you be abandoned to the score. Let your piety be so secret that even you don't know you're doing it: let it be for God's eyes only. Abandon yourself to the music of his mercy.

Jesus is offering us a where, why, how of spirituality. Where do we commune with God? In secret. Why do we commune with God? To please him. How do we commune with God? As Father. A lifetime of spiritual adventure could be built on these three simple questions.

2. JUST DESERTS

Location *Matthew 6:5-8.* And when you pray, do not be like the hypocrites, for they love to pray standing in the synagogues and on the street corners to be seen by men. I tell you the truth, they have received their reward in full. But when you pray, go into your room, close the door and pray to your Father, who is unseen. Then your Father, who sees what is done in secret, will reward you. And when you pray, do not keep on babbling like pagans, for they think they will be heard because of their many words. Do not be like them, for your Father knows what you need before you ask him.'

Landmarks Prayer – it ain't what you say, it's the way you don't say it. Making the conversation two-way. Finding your desert place of prayer.

What to see Carlo Carretto was a Catholic priest who, in the years following the Second World War, rose through the church's hierarchy. He became the Director of Catholic Action, a global youth movement with genuine clout in the church. With a high profile Vatican office, he was the very definition of a mover and shaker in the post-war church. 'Then, when I was forty-four years old', he writes, 'there occurred the most serious call of my life: the call to the contemplative life. I experienced it deeply – in the depth which only faith can provide and where darkness is absolute – where human strength can no longer help. This time I had to say 'yes' without understanding a thing. "Leave everything and come with me into the desert. It is not your acts and deeds that I want; I want your prayer, your love."'[57]

Carretto joined a monastic order and moved to the deserts of North Africa, where he tried 'to place myself, naked, poor and alone, in the presence of God's eternal majesty, totally committed to penetrating the logic of the Gospels, which is inexhaustible.'[58] He writes movingly of the moment, not long into his desert experience, when he broke 'the last tie with the past'. The thick notebook he had carried for years contained the contact details of his thousands of friends

the world over. Making a small fire behind a dune, he burned the book page by page. He writes, 'I can still see the black ashes of the notebook being swept away into the distance by the wind of the Sahara.'[59] This was the decisive moment at which he was cut off from his former life of activity and ambition. With the address book destroyed, Carretto records that he 'never loved nor prayed so much for my old friends as in the solitude of the desert.'[60]

Though Carretto returned from the desert some ten years later and took up a more public life once more, he never went back to his former drivenness. His story is an acted parable of the principles Jesus is proposing here. Prayer, like giving, is not about public performance but private perseverance. It is an inner journey, along roads on which God alone is our guide. For Carretto, the difference was physical and geographical. God led him into a new context on a new continent in order to teach him to pray. For others, the contrast may be less visible, and less extreme. But it must be there all the same. I came across Carretto's *Letters from the Desert* as a recently converted teenager. Though God never called me to the desert itself, the experience of this Italian priest many years my senior spoke to me of the 'desert of the heart'. I came to understand the need to create a place of peace and solitude in my life, a place in which I could be silent before God; where activity and accolades meant nothing. Time and time again in the years since this discovery,

God has called me back to this place. 'The cure for too-much-to-do', writes Dallas Willard, 'is solitude and silence, for there you find you are safely more than what you do. And the cure for loneliness is solitude and silence, for there you discover in how many ways you are never alone.'[61]

The place of prayer to which Jesus is calling us is this place of solitude and silence – far away from the 'pray and display' of performed piety. If we understand nothing else of prayer, we must understand that it is a cultivation of the inner life. 'We must understand the connection between inner solitude and inner silence; they are inseparable. All the masters of the interior life speak of the two in the same breath.'[62] Jesus is not suggesting that prayer should never be a public or corporate act: but he is saying that the engine-room of prayer, the wellsprings of spirituality, lie in the private relationship with God. Think of a deeply rooted tree. There is growth above ground level, but the life is drawn from the roots.

This life of private prayer would have come as a radical new idea to many of Jesus' first listeners. The public expression of prayer had become so dominant in Jewish life, with a strong emphasis on the Temple, and on the professional role of the priest, that many 'ordinary believers' saw little in it for themselves. They were pawns in the religious game, pushed from pillar to post by a priestly élite on the one hand and a distant, dangerous God on the other. This has become the norm in every culture in which religion has been formalised, ritualised, complicated and handed over to a hierarchy of professional operatives. The only antidote is the growth of real spirituality in the cultivation of the hidden life of prayer. Where do we commune with God? In secret. Why do we commune with God? To please him. How do we commune with God? As father.

DISTRICT 3: SPIRITUAL

What to do

■ Reflect on the when and where of prayer in your life. Jesus suggests going 'into your room', but this can mean different things for different people. For some there is a special place set aside; others will take a walk outdoors. Some will sense the presence of God most in chapels or sacred places. Find out what the best case scenario is for you, then consider how you could be in that scenario more often!

■ Explore silence and quiet in prayer. Kill any tendency to babble at God, reeling off a list of needs like a shopping list dictated to Tesco. Experiment with the art of listening in prayer.

Places to stay

Leave empty things to empty-minded people, and direct your thoughts to God's commands for you. Shut the door upon yourself, and invite in Jesus, your beloved. Stay with him in your cell, for you will not find peace like that elsewhere. *Thomas à Kempis*[63]

Retirement is the laboratory of the soul: interior solitude and silence are its two wings. All great works are prepared in the desert, including the redemption of the world. *A.G. Sertillanges*[64]

R E T R O - T O U R

And when thou prayest, thou shalt not be as the hypocrites are: for they love to pray standing in the synagogues and in the corners of the streets, that they may be seen of men. Verily I say unto you, They have their reward. But thou, when thou prayest, enter into thy closet, and when thou hast shut thy door, pray to thy Father which is in secret; and thy Father which seeth in secret shall reward thee openly. But when ye pray, use not vain repetitions, as the heathen do: for they think that they shall be heard for their much speaking. Be not ye therefore like unto them: for your Father knoweth what things ye have need of, before ye ask him.

DISTRICT 3: SPIRITUAL

You may be fond of praying in public or in a group. Corporate worship may mean the world to you. But your inner life will only ever be as deep as it is when you are alone.

SUBWAY MAP

STATION
1 Kings 19:3-18 – Elijah finds renewal in the desert experience.
Psalm 78:13-31 – God's provision in desert places.

CONNECTIONS
Matthew 4:1-11,
Matthew 26:36-46 – the prayer life of Jesus, in the desert and the garden.

3. Yourkingdom.com

Location *Matthew 6:9-10.* This, then, is how you should pray: 'Our Father in heaven, hallowed be your name, your kingdom come, your will be done on earth as it is in heaven.'

Landmarks 'Our Father': an opening gambit or a life long quest? God's homepage to kick-start your spiritual surfing.

What to see Having established the context in which he wants to deal with prayer – that it looks for the secret place, addresses God alone and is founded in relationship with the Father – Jesus goes on to explore the content of prayer in more depth. 'The Lord's Prayer' or the 'Our Father' is the best known of all Christian prayers, not least because it is given to us by Jesus. It has been used through the history of the Church in a number of ways. For some, the words themselves have value, so that 'saying the Lord's prayer' becomes significant. Others have taken it as a framework, using its separate phrases as a kind of menu through which to pray each day. Still others still see it as a map marking out the wider territories of prayer – a guide to the things we should be praying about. All three approaches can be helpful and fruitful, and you will probably find yourself drawn to each on different occasions. There is very little about prayer that cannot legitimately find shelter under this umbrella. Just as the tallest of oak trees is contained in an acorn so these few phrases capture, in essence, the breadth of Christian prayer.

The prayer is founded on the triple statement of this first phrase: it is a statement of who God is, of where God is and of what God is doing.

Who God is

In the film *Ransom*, Mel Gibson plays an airline tycoon whose son is kidnapped. In one of the script's most tense moments, Gibson's desperation for his lost son overwhelms him as he shouts down a telephone to the kidnappers he cannot see, 'Give me back my son!' The pain and passion etched into the wounded father's face bring the drama of the entire film into razor-sharp focus.

When Yahweh sends Moses to confront Pharaoh, he sends him with the same impassioned message, 'Israel is my firstborn son. ... let my son go'.[65] The Exodus God, the God who comes to liberate and heal, the God who is the source and strength of the kingdom announcement Jesus brings, is the God who is our Father. Our Father because he is the Father of all – the Creator and Sustainer of the universe. Father because of all the dimensions in which we could know him, of all the images available, his greatest desire is that we should know him as parent.

No other name of God or image of God captures more fully the purpose of salvation. God wants to be our perfect parent.

Where God is

To place God in Heaven at the outset of this prayer serves two distinct purposes. The first is that it leaves the hearer in no doubt that this is the supreme God, the God who is over all. The gods before Yahweh were local gods, owned by a particular tribe or limited to a particular place. They could be powerful and frightening when you stood close to them, but they lost their power if you moved away. Yahweh, by contrast, is the God above all gods, the God who is so powerful that he cannot give an earthly address. All of creation is not big enough to contain him: he is over and above the cosmos. This links to the second purpose for locating God in this way, in that it lays the foundation for our prayers. Our prayer is valid because the God to whom we pray is in a position to answer us. From his high vantage point, he sees all and knows all. We can be confident that the currency of our prayer has real value. This is no mere sergeant major. It is to the commander-in-chief of the armies of heaven that our petition is addressed. Prayer is like a penthouse lift – it goes straight to the top.

What God is doing

There are several biblical words whose usage, over the years, has strayed from their original contexts. One of these is the word heaven. In contemporary language, heaven is used almost exclusively to describe the future eternal home of the saints – it is inextricably tied up with the after-life. This is not the case in the New Testament. Here, 'heaven' is rarely used to describe a destination but far more often as a source. Heaven is the dwelling place of God, from which the promised reign of blessing – the kingdom – is being released. When we pray 'your kingdom come, your will be done on earth as it is in heaven', we are capturing the direction of the blessing of God. It is from heaven to earth that the kingdom flows. The consummation of this hope is described by the Apostle John in his Revelation in these words, 'I saw … the new Jerusalem coming down out of heaven from God, … and I heard a loud voice from the throne saying, "Now the dwelling place of God is with men…"'[66] Whatever God has planned for us in the future, there is a direction to the kingdom that goes from the courts of heaven to the created order.

Places to stay

We live, as Jesus lived, in a world all too full of injustice, hunger, malice and evil. This prayer cries out for justice, bread, forgiveness and deliverance. If anyone thinks those are irrelevant in today's world, let them read the newspaper and think again. *Tom Wright*[67]

Before we can pray 'Thy kingdom come', we must be willing to pray 'My kingdom go'. *Alan Redpath*[68]

R E T R O - T O U R

After this manner therefore pray ye: Our Father which art in heaven, Hallowed be thy name. Thy kingdom come, Thy will be done in earth, as it is in heaven.

God is in the business of pouring out blessing on the earth. The kingdom is heaven@earth.com.

These three realities form the foundations on which the Lord's Prayer is constructed. It is because of who God is that we can approach him in the first place. He knows us. He is the perfect parent who has already initiated our rescue, our Exodus. He is for us. It is because of where God is that we can pray in confidence. His cheques will never bounce. He has the position and the power to back up his promise to us. He is the highest authority. And it is because of what God is doing that our prayers have meaning. He is already engaged in releasing blessing from heaven to the earth. No problem we bring to him is beyond his scope. We are asking him to do what he is already committed to doing.

4. OUR DAILY BREATH

Location *Matthew 6:11-12.* Give us today our daily bread. Forgive us our debts, as we also have forgiven our debtors.

Landmarks Our needs and God's provision: an experience for the everyday. Forgiveness given and received: a reality as intimate as breathing.

What to see When political upheaval erupted in Albania in the 1990s, the population had a unique way of measuring the depth of the crisis. Already among

Europe's poorest people, the Albanians knew the value of bread in their daily lives, and as long as they had bread they could survive. The point at which mass panic broke out was the point at which there was no bread in the shops. For these people, the availability of daily bread was the one, irrefutable measure of economic stability. Bread, for the poor, is survival.

The prayer for daily bread sets out starkly the parameters by which our needs are brought to God.

■ Firstly, it tells us to bring real needs, not a shopping-list of wants. Our God is not a sugar daddy, programmed to deliver every toy and trinket our neurotic minds could wish for. He is committed, rather, to our health and growth, to our development as his human creatures. He wants to give us that which will sustain us.

■ Secondly, it tells us to bring 'daily' needs. This concept is further developed later in the Sermon, when Jesus tells us that 'each day has enough trouble of its own'. This is a remarkable cure for neurosis and anxiety that the best therapist can't match. It is extraordinarily helpful to ask yourself 'what do I need today?' – not just in terms of physical bread, but also of other needs and outcomes. To focus on the coming 24 hours is to give concrete reality to the act of praying.

■ Thirdly, it reiterates the corporate nature of this prayer. The 'our' of our Father now becomes the 'our' of need. Who is the 'us' on whose behalf we pray? The only answer that does justice to the context and the wider New Testament ethos is the 'us' of humanity. When we pray for bread, we stand shoulder to shoulder with those who have none. Our very sharp sense of our own need is tempered by our awareness of the needs of others. And though we might spiritualise the meaning of 'bread' in our own lives to cover a wide range of needs and outcomes, we remember that for much of the population of our planet the need remains for real, physical, edible bread.

If our needs are to be dealt with on a daily basis, so too is our forgiveness. There is no direct link between verses 11 and 12, other than that they appear together as the heart of this prayer, but there is an implication of a daily pattern. It is as if the 'big question' of forgiveness properly belongs alongside the 'ordinary question' of bread. Certainly, in my own reading and use of the prayer, I have tended to let the daily pattern of the prayer for bread spill over into the prayer for forgiveness. What do I need forgiven today? Who do I need to forgive today? Just as dealing with needs in 24-hour blocks heads off anxiety, so keeping short accounts in the realm of forgiveness is wisdom of the highest order. The apostle Paul reflects this in his advice to 'not let the sun go down while you are still angry'[69]

There are two aspects of this petition for forgiveness that should help us to live in its light.

Forgiveness and forgiving are linked

This is one of the few places in which Jesus appears to place conditions on grace. Not only does the prayer itself link the two, but immediately after it Jesus makes the point again. 'If you forgive...'[70] Is this our forgiveness of others leading to our forgiveness by God, or is it the receipt of forgiveness flowing out in the offer of forgiveness? The honest answer is that both are implied. What Jesus is saying seems to be:

■ that the word 'forgiveness' describes both giving and receiving – just as 'breathing' implies both inhaling and exhaling. There is a moment of birth when only the first happens and a moment of death when it is only the last: but at all points in between the two are inseparable, and the word covers both. To breathe is to be alive. To be forgiven is to forgive.

■ that the inner release that comes from receiving forgiveness is not complete until forgiveness is offered. This is not a statement of God's intent, but of human reality. The one who refuses to forgive remains, in a very real sense, imprisoned. That God forgives us is a miracle – that he gives us power to forgive is equally so. 'There is a hard law ... that when a deep injury is done to us, we never recover until we forgive.'[71]

■ that the offer of forgiveness to others is the evidence of forgiveness received. The fruit indicates the root. We are forgiven when grace comes into our lives: that we forgive is the outworking of its presence.

Forgiveness is comprehensive

The kingdom announcement of absolute grace insists that there is nothing for which we cannot be forgiven. The Hebrew concept of 'sin' includes the sense of 'failure to fulfil a duty'. It is not only our deliberate acts of rebellion against the Creator for which we need forgiveness, but also the more general sense in which we have failed to meet our obligations. This also sets the measure with which we forgive others. We forgive not only those who have deliberately and directly hurt us, but also those who have simply let us down. Even, if we are to make grace absolute, those by whom we feel let down. The list of those you might name in this

act of forgiveness will grow considerably if you include those additional people: but there is no better way to ensure that resentment never finds the soil to grow in. 'Don't give the devil a foothold'[72] is Paul's advice: and forgiveness – even for the most trivial of offences – is the key.

It is important to note that this whole discussion of forgiveness takes place in the context of prayer, which we have already described as being in the secret place, for God alone and founded on the fatherhood of God. There may be times where forgiveness has to be spoken out – to the person in question and perhaps more widely. But that is not what Jesus is speaking of here. This, rather, is about forgiveness before God and in the heart: where the battle begins. Start with the heart, and let God guide you after that as to whether some other action is needed.

DISTRICT 3: SPIRITUAL

What to do

■ **Begin today**. Take a fresh look at the Lord's Prayer and decide what difference it might make to your prayer life – whether as words you use, as a framework you adopt or as an inspiration to guide your wider prayers.

■ **Begin today**. Think about what needs you should bring to God today, not only for yourself but for others. Make a mental note – or a written list if you prefer – and bring these needs to God. Make a commitment to refresh the list tomorrow, and pray again.

■ **Begin today**. Repeat this process with forgiveness. Bring to mind all the things you need to ask forgiveness for, and also all the people you need to forgive. Include any towards whom you have begun to feel resentment, even if you're not sure what they have done to deserve it. In prayer, release them from their debt.

Places to stay

It is our birthright, as followers of Jesus, to breathe in true divine forgiveness day by day, as the cool, clean air which our spiritual lungs need.... And once we start inhaling God's fresh air, there is a good chance that we will start to breathe it out, too. As we learn what it is like to be forgiven, we begin to discover that it is possible, and indeed joyful, to forgive others. *Tom Wright*[73]

It is freeing to become aware that we do not have to be victims of our past and can learn new ways of responding. But there is a step beyond this recognition... It is the step of forgiveness. Forgiveness is love practised among people who love poorly. It sets us free without wanting anything in return. *Henri Nouwen*[74]

R E T R O · T O U R

Give us this day our daily bread. And forgive us our debts, as we forgive our debtors.

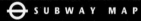 SUBWAY MAP

STATION
Proverbs 30:7-9 – 'daily bread' defined.

CONNECTIONS
John 6:25-59 – Jesus the bread of life.

5. MAPPING THE MINEFIELD

Location *Matthew 6:13-15*. And lead us not into temptation, but deliver us from the evil one. For if you forgive men when they sin against you, your heavenly Father will also forgive you. But if you do not forgive men their sins, your Father will not forgive your sins.

Landmarks The leading of God as a positive experience. Forgiveness as the power to disarm evil, one booby-trapped bomb at a time.

What to see There are a number of passages in the Bible which, when I was young, I found bizarre to the point of obscurity. This is one of them. Why on earth would God want to lead us into temptation, so much so that we need to ask him not to? Why do we have to beg God not to tempt us? What kind of God is it that has to be persuaded not to harm us? I could never understand how millions of Christians could pray this prayer each week, if not each day, without asking themselves this question. I could not accept then, and I cannot now, that Jesus could be who he said he was if that is the kind of God he came to announce.

My problem of course is that I was placing the emphasis of this sentence in the wrong place. By seeing the word 'not' at the heart of the equation, I construed the sentence in the negative – as a request to God not to do something he might otherwise be inclined to do. But the emphasis of the sentence is positive. The accent should be on the word 'lead'.

Consider the journey of any contemporary of Jesus forced to travel between cities. On any given stretch of road, say between Jerusalem and Jericho, there were a range of risks and hazards, especially at night. The road itself could contain potholes and other dangers, which were easy to miss if your concentration momentarily slipped. Then there was the possibility of attack by robbers, a regular occurrence dramatised by Jesus in the parable of the Good Samaritan.[75] There were other dangers: the danger of mistiming your journey, and ending up without shelter at night; the danger of getting lost along the way; the danger posed by wild animals or unwanted travelling companions. An unexpected change in the weather could make your journey uncomfortable or even impossible. First century travellers knew that no journey was without its perils and pitfalls. The fortunate traveller was the one who had a reliable guide: someone who knew the region and the road, who was alert and attentive, who could read the signs of the climate. To travel with such a guide was to travel safely.

This is the role we are inviting God to play in our lives. 'If you lead us, Father', we are saying, 'we will not fall into the many pitfalls on our route'. Whether you translate the term used here as 'temptation' or 'trial' or as 'do not lead us to the time of testing', the impact is the same. It is the cry to God to lead us in such

a way as to keep us safe and on the right road. Perhaps the clearest contemporary equivalent would be the image of crossing a mine-field – and trusting God because he alone knows where the mines are. There are a number of important themes wrapped up in this petition:

We need our God to lead us

The relationship we are here praying for is not one in which God sets us on our route, then leaves us to it, but one in which we depend, moment by moment, on his guiding hand. The implication is clear: the more completely we trust in God's leading, the more fully we will be safe from trial and harm.

God's ways are the ways that lead to life

The wisdom tradition of the Old Testament, contained in the books of Proverbs and Ecclesiastes and reflected in the Psalms and Prophets, was built on the idea that God's laws were the key to health and life. By following the revealed ways of God, the devout person would experience shalom, a deep personal peace and prosperity. God's ways were revealed not just for the cultic life of the Temple, but for the whole of life, from seeking honesty amongst neighbours to giving good measure in the market-place. There is something of the same tradition here, in the idea that the ways of God are the ways of life. 'Lead us, Father, and we will know shalom in our lives'.

DISTRICT 3: SPIRITUAL

DISTRICT 3: SPIRITUAL

What to do

■ Reconnect with God's leading. Consider when it last was that you really experienced the leading of God. What can you do to refresh the sense of that leading as a daily experience?

■ Seek out God's wisdom. Reflect on the areas of your life in which you have not been in the habit of seeking the wisdom of God. Consider what it might mean for you to do so.

■ Ask for God's help in identifying the areas of temptation and trial to which you are particularly vulnerable. What are the areas of weakness that you need to steer clear of?

Father, I confess my total need of you. The road is hard and dangerous, and the night is dark. I travel safely only if you travel at my side. Be with me, I pray – guide me, direct my steps, speak to me. And teach me, Father, both to listen and to obey.

There is more to Christianity than creeds

If it is true that the ways of God are the ways that lead to life and that the wisdom of God is available to us, then it should follow that our lives will show signs of the blessing of God. This is not just for the religious realm. In every area of life, there should be marks of wholeness and shalom. This does not mean that to be a Christian is to live the perfect life – but it does mean that the adventure of following Jesus is a journey into wholeness in every sense. The Christian gospel should recommend itself to seekers on the evidence of the lives of those already following it.

The final clause of this verse, and of the prayer, gives the answer to the question,

'When should we stop praying?' The goal of our life of prayer is this: to be delivered from the very presence of evil. This is no less than the total reversal of the fall, as we look to a cosmos returned once more to the plans of God. The 'us' here must, once again, be the 'us' of humanity. When does prayer end? When every corner of the earth has been swept clean of evil. When the distortion brought by the fall is utterly healed. Until this day – the promised 'Day of God' – we are duty-bound to go on praying; in the words of Tom Wright, 'standing in the presence of the pain of the world, and kneeling in the presence of the Creator of the world.'[76] As if to remind us that this is not some detached spiritual activity far from the rigours of the real world, Jesus reiterates the call to forgive. If the aim of the kingdom is to sweep the

Places to stay

Opportunity may only knock once – but temptation leans on the bell. *Anon*

Today we, the children of Western culture, post-modern, adult children of the enlightenment, struggle with practical atheism. Our churches are slowly emptying and, more and more, the sense of God is slipping from our ordinary lives... The road back to a lively faith is not a question of finding the right answers, but of living a certain way, contemplatively. The existence of God, like the air we breathe, need not be proven. It is more a question of developing good lungs to meet it correctly... We must live in such a way as to give birth to God in our lives. *Ronald Rolheiser*[77]

R E T R O · T O U R

And lead us not into temptation, but deliver us from evil: For thine is the kingdom, and the power, and the glory, for ever. Amen. For if ye forgive men their trespasses, your heavenly Father will also forgive you: But if ye forgive not men their trespasses, neither will your Father forgive your trespasses.

cosmos clear of evil, it is forgiveness from which the bristles of the brush are made. The frontline of the kingdom is the place where forgiveness is at work. If temptation and evil in the world can be represented as a minefield, forgiveness is the clearance programme, disarming the powers one mine at a time.

⊖ S U B W A Y M A P

STATION
Deuteronomy 30:11-20 – the law of God offered as the path to fullness of life.
Psalm 23 – God's faithful leading pictured in the work of a shepherd

CONNECTIONS
John 10:1-10 – Jesus as the shepherd, leading us to abundant life.

6. PHYSICAL GRAFFITI

Location *Matthew 6:16-18.* When you fast, do not look sombre as the hypocrites do, for they disfigure their faces to show men they are fasting. I tell you the truth, they have received their reward in full. But when you fast, put oil on your head and wash your face, so that it will not be obvious to men that you are fasting, but only to your Father, who is unseen; and your Father, who sees what is done in secret, will reward you.

Landmarks Life in the fasting lane: the lost art of prayer made physical. Why fasting works. Abstaining without complaining – how going without can be a source of joy.

What to see For the third and final time, Jesus' theme words are repeated – hypocrites, reward, secret and Father. Once again the model of spirituality which is private, for God's benefit and founded on relationship with the Father is proposed, this time in the context of fasting. Jesus makes no attempt to say that fasting will not be a part of his new, non-legalistic spirituality – only that it has no place as a performance art. True fasting – the fasting that only God sees – is still encouraged.

There are three things about fasting that bear mentioning in this context:

■ **Fasting works**. There can be no doubt that fasting, properly practised, has significant benefits in the hidden life of prayer. It sharpens the focus of prayer and clears the mind. It brings, very often, a heightened awareness of the presence and purposes of God. It opens new doors of creativity.

■ **Fasting is good for you**. Even apart from all its spiritual and emotional impact, fasting has significant physical benefits. It is a Sabbath-rest for the body, and allows for all manner of restoration and repair. Most people who include fasting as a regular part of their lives speak of its significant benefits.

■ **Fasting has pedigree**. As a spiritual discipline, fasting is probably the oldest and most proven companion to prayer. Christians have practised it for centuries, and many other faiths also do so. Because eating has so central and fundamental a role in human life, fasting touches us at a very deep level, in the commonness of our humanity.

The wider significance of Jesus' endorsement of the practice of fasting is that it legitimises the physical realm of spiritual experience. Fasting is physical prayer – it is praying not with thoughts and words alone, but with the disposition of our bodies. The benefits of fasting arise from the clear and well-documented relationship of physiological and spiritual well-being. This is an area in which Eastern and New Age practices are sometimes ahead of the modern church, which in many ways has over-verbalised and over-intellectualised its faith. The same principle applies to posture and movement, both of which have a role to play in spirituality. The rediscovery of a Christian spirituality that embraces the physical dimension is one of the welcome signs of the Church's engagement with post-modern culture.

Jesus' handling of the place of fasting effectively switches it from a negative experience of deprivation to a positive experience of the life of God. He rejects entirely the point scoring misery of the visibly deprived devotee, and suggests that those who fast should use a little oil and fresh water to look even better than normal. There is a sense here of celebration, of fasting as a kind of spiritual dance. If it not about joy and the benefits of knowing God, if it is not doing you good, stop doing it. No one is impressed by your self-imposed agony.

It has become fashionable in our own age to substitute other forms of voluntary abstinence for the more traditional idea of going without food. Some talk of fasting from television, from alcohol or from sex. There are doubtless great benefits in any and all of these, but it has to be said that the teaching given here does not indicate them. Fasting was taken in Jesus' day to mean abstinence from food, and that has been its primary meaning over the centuries. This arises almost certainly from the recognition that of all the human appetites, the appetite for food is central. Many of us only discover just how central it is when we first attempt to fast. What seems at first as though it should be an easy task – the gentle uphill stroll of a day or half-day without food – becomes, within hours, the climbing of a sheer rock face. We are not aware of the power food has over us because in our everyday experience we are rarely deprived of it. If this is true for you, it is probably the only argument you need to adopt fasting as a regular discipline. If it achieves nothing more than the breaking of the stranglehold of food on your life, it will have done you a great service.

DISTRICT 3: SPIRITUAL

What to do

■ Rewind and Review. Have you attempted a fast? Did you make it through? What were the benefits for you? Where there is good fruit, consider how you can bring this practice more fully into your ongoing routine.

■ Get a face-lift. Fasting or not, are you someone whose spirituality speaks of joy and celebration to those around you, or someone whose face spells misery? Consider what you might do to lighten the weight of the spirituality you carry with you.

■ Fast forward. Consider what place fasting might have for you in the future. If you want to bring it more centrally into your spirituality, plan to do so incrementally: moving from half-day fasts, to days, to longer periods. The two patterns most common in Christian history are the commitment to a weekly one day fast or the pursuit of longer fasts on a less frequent basis, associated with special times of prayer and renewal.

DISTRICT 3: SPIRITUAL

Places to stay

Fasting helps to express, to deepen and to confirm the resolution that we are ready to sacrifice anything – to sacrifice ourselves – to attain what we seek for the kingdom of God. *Andrew Murray*[78]

Some people's religion is like a wooden leg. There is neither warmth nor life in it, and although it helps them hobble along, it never becomes part of them, and must be strapped on each morning. *Anon*[79]

R E T R O · T O U R

Moreover when ye fast, be not, as the hypocrites, of a sad countenance: for they disfigure their faces, that they may appear unto men to fast. Verily I say unto you, They have their reward. But thou, when thou fastest, anoint thine head, and wash thy face; That thou appear not unto men to fast, but unto thy Father which is in secret: and thy Father, which seeth in secret, shall reward thee openly.

There are three questions that have formed the framework of our exploration of Jesus' post-legalistic spirituality: where do we commune with God? – in secret. Why do we commune with God? – to please him. How do we commune with God? – as Father. These same three questions can help us to evaluate the benefits of fasting. If fasting helps enables to cultivate your inner life, if it brings you closer to God, if it becomes an experience of joy shared with your Father, then you will know that it is taking you down the roads that it should. If, on the other hand, the practice only serves to make you miserable and impose your misery on those around you, you should perhaps look again at how and why you have adopted it. A journalist once defined Puritanism as 'the haunting fear that someone, somewhere may be happy' – don't let the ancient art of fasting send that kind of message to your peers.

SUBWAY MAP

STATION
Isaiah 58:1-14 – A powerful description of the true fasting that God looks for in his people.

CONNECTIONS
Luke 4:1-13 – Jesus own experience of the battles and benefits of fasting:
Luke 4:18-19 – Jesus' self-declaration of the nature of the kingdom announcement, following his forty day fast.

Tourist information Panel

TIP 5 – Local Faiths

There were a number of competing religious traditions in Palestine in the first century. The foremost of these was Hellenism – a kind of open, non-demanding religion centred around the worship of a whole cluster of gods. Some of these gods offered health, wisdom, beauty, love, prosperity whilst others symbolised justice and protection. The Roman development of the religion brought the gods into the house and each villa would have an altar to their household gods – the Lares and Penates. So Greek and Roman religion was about a community's offering of worship rather than a personal commitment to one god or one system of faith.

Judaism was completely different. Arising from the experience of the Hebrew people, their persecution in Egypt, their liberation by Yahweh through his prophet Moses and the various covenants which Yahweh made with them over the subsequent centuries, Judaism was all about a relationship with one God, Yahweh. Israel was God's people, his chosen race. Central to the Jewish understanding was this covenantal relationship – God promised to care for his people and look after them, to

bring them salvation. On the other hand to show that they lived within this covenant, God's people had to follow his commands and live according to sacred texts handed down through prophets and others – especially Moses. Shortcomings in this covenant were overcome by the use of sacrifice and prayer, focused on the Temple in Jerusalem, the authorised place of worship – the place where God was supposed to be found.

The two religions existed alongside one another in Galilee at the time of Jesus. Jewish settlers had been sent to the region a hundred years before in order to make the area more Jewish. However, scholars are still unsure how Jewish Galilee would have been: after all it was still known as Galilee of the Gentiles, i.e. Galilee of the non-Jews. It may be that the area was not a hotbed of Jewish spirituality but rather a mixed multicultural region offering a number of religious lifestyles and persuasions.

Tourist information Panel

TIP 6 – Local Piety

Almsgiving, fasting and prayer

In Isaiah 58:6ff God suggests the ingredients of true worship:

"Is not this the kind of fasting I have chosen: to loose the chains of injustice and untie the cords of the yoke, to set the oppressed free and break every yoke? Is it not to share your food with the hungry and to provide the poor wanderer with shelter – when you see the naked, to clothe him, and not to turn away from your own flesh and blood? Then your light will break forth like the dawn, and your healing will quickly appear; then your righteousness will go before you, and the glory of the LORD will be your rear guard. Then you will call, and the LORD will answer; you will cry for help, and he will say: Here am I."

Throughout the Bible worship and justice go hand in hand. To cry for justice and to seek to bring about justice and equality are an act of worship in themselves. As in Isaiah 58, worship is actually something you do as part of your lifestyle – not just singing songs and saying prayers and listening to sermons in church. In Jewish tradition as in the Sermon on the Mount, three basic actions are referred to as acts of worship – almsgiving, prayer and fasting.

For a Jew to give alms meant any kind of action that reflected God's covenant love. In the Wisdom of Sirach it is seen as the most acceptable form of worship because it doesn't take anything away from the poor. Almsgiving included giving to the poor but also visiting the sick, showing hospitality to strangers, outfitting a bride who couldn't afford a wedding, accompanying the dead and the dying, even offering regular prayer. In other words, almsgiving meant giving something of yourself to someone else: offering back to God through someone else something of the life that he had given to you.

Fasting was common practice in both Jewish and Greek worship. In Judaism it was a sign of mourning and penitence as well as a means of concentrating the mind. Fasting could be for a long or short period and also could either be partial or total. What was important was that the worshipper should focus upon God rather than the external effects of fasting.

DISTRICT 3: SPIRITUAL

DISTRICT 4: FINANCIAL
Of Trust and Rust
Matthew 6:19 - 7:14

Orientation and information

Visit any major city of the world in the early morning or late afternoon, and you will see the equivalent of a river in flood. Like overflowing drains, the tributaries of a thousand side streets disgorge vehicles and pedestrians into the powerful currents of the main thoroughfares. People, cars, trains and buses flow together to and from the heart of the city. In the morning hours, there is an inflow; by evening an outflow. Both are illuminated, when the light is poor, by the coursing choreography of a million tail lights.

The focus of this daily mass migration can be captured in one word: work. While the inner-city ring, the suburbs and the greenbelt beyond function primarily, for a significant number of people, as home, the heart of the city is more easily associated with employment, and the exchange of skills for money. At the very core of the crowds, in almost every case, you will find the financial district. This hive of activity and industry serves to create and manage capital, to provide insurance and investment advice, to drive profits and generate wealth. Connected invisibly by a million modems – and visibly by the constant exchange of paper – the heartbeat of this district sets the pace for the whole nation. Power and prestige are proclaimed in the glass and chrome palaces that scrape the sky: emblems of empire and excess.

At the foot of these great towers, bars, restaurants and cafés compete for the patronage of the power-brokers, and provide tables at which deals can be done. Here there is movement and activity, the busyness of doing business. The blood that flows through this eco-system is money; the measure of its prosperity and the mark of its power. Humans will work for it, fight for it, live for it and die for it, and as they pile it high around themselves, their souls are satisfied with the fruits of their lives....

Or not, Jesus says. Just as he would later storm into the Temple courts and give the money changers a new understanding of turnover, so here he strides into the financial concerns at the heart of the city of our lives and challenges the assumptions we have made. 'Where is your heart?', he asks us, 'What is your focus?' Are you sweating your life away for profits and property that is destined for dust? Or is there another way? Is it possible our heartbeat might not be money, but life? Can we resist the power and attraction of the glass and chrome gods, and build a different kind of city?

These questions speak of aspirations that have been known to humanity since the first stone axe merchant bartered beans with the first stone axe buyer, and the inventor of the wheel signed a distribution contract with UgggFord. They dominated the lives of rich and poor in the days of Jesus, and they dominate our lives today. Then, as now, the answers Jesus offers are as radical as a safe without a lock.

HIGHLIGHTS

- The eyes have it
- High anxiety
- Here comes the judge
- Knock, knock, whose heir?
- Limited luggage allowance

1. THE EYES HAVE IT

Location *Matthew 6:19-24*. Do not store up for yourselves treasures on earth, where moth and rust destroy, and where thieves break in and steal. But store up for yourselves treasures in heaven, where moth and rust do not destroy, and where thieves do not break in and steal. For where your treasure is, there your heart will be also. The eye is the lamp of the body. If your eyes are good, your whole body will be full of light. But if your eyes are bad, your whole body will be full of darkness. If then the light within you is darkness, how great is that darkness! No-one can serve two masters. Either he will hate the one and love the other, or he will be devoted to the one and despise the other. You cannot serve both God and Money.

Landmarks Jesus proposes a WYSIWYG [What You See is What You Get] lifestyle. We look to God to be the measure of simplicity and the mainstay of security.

What to see A central question in our grasp of the Sermon on the Mount is 'What time is it?'. The question refers not to the actual time at which Jesus spoke these words – which is unknown to us – but to the time frame within which the call to 'store up treasures in heaven' is set. Christian tradition has tended to see heaven as a future reality, so that we are being asked here to defer gratification now so as to enjoy a reward in the future. We are to resist the temptation to store up for ourselves consumer durables, fine wines, Star Wars memorabilia and every other good thing, so that in due course our post-resurrection pad will be the envy of all our friends. Obedience to such a call requires teeth-gritting discipline and patience, and the maturity to live with the silence of God while we wait for his response.

But is that really what Jesus is asking of us? To his Jewish audience, it would not be. Heaven for the Hebrew was not a future state of bliss, but the present place of God's dwelling: the throne-room from which his will and purposes flow out. We are not being asked to defer or delay our aspirations so much as to access a totally different and currently available economy. This is not a choice between live now and live later, so much as an invitation to live differently. Our treasure in heaven can be accessed in the now, because heaven, in Christ, is made accessible. Our efforts to live out the new humanity to which Jesus calls us are backed by the ready resources of heaven. The freedom to choose lifestyle options that are not connected to material, social or cultural success seems to be a hallmark of the kingdom, and is linked by Jesus to a deep sense of fullness and completion. It is not the immediate

What to do

Examine your heart. What do you desire? Spend time writing an honest list of the things you really want, across all areas of your life. Wrestle with yourself and with God to shape this list. How many of these desires are legitimately part of your walk with God, and how many are simply your 'wish list'? Ask God what items on your list you should give priority to, and where you should invest to bring them to fruition.

Rest your eyes. For a month, make a habit of either leaving the room or switching your TV off whenever adverts are on, especially where they are for products you crave. After a month, see if your spending habits have been impacted.

Take a retreat. Whether alone or with a guide, take time-out to reassess the priorities of your life. Examine just where it is that you are investing time, energy and resources and ask why. Look for more creative and imaginative ways to use all three.

Break Mammon's power. Identify a possession that means a lot to you, something that would fit the description of 'treasure' in your life. Give it away.

Places to stay

O thou who art wisdom and pity both, set me free from the lordship of desire. Help me to find my happiness in my acceptance of my purpose: in friendly eyes; in work well done; in quietness born of trust, and most of all, in the awareness of your presence in my spirit. *Celtic Prayer*[81]

Just as science has found the power of the sun itself to be locked in the atom, so religion proclaims the glory of the eternal to be reflected in the simplest elements of time: a leaf, a door, an unturned stone. *Huton Smith*[82]

R E T R O · T O U R

Lay not up for yourselves treasures upon earth, where moth and rust doth corrupt, and where thieves break through and steal: But lay up for yourselves treasures in heaven, where neither moth nor rust doth corrupt, and where thieves do not break through nor steal: For where your treasure is, there will your heart be also. The light of the body is the eye: if therefore thine eye be single, thy whole body shall be full of light. But if thine eye be evil, thy whole body shall be full of darkness. If therefore the light that is in thee be darkness, how great is that darkness! No man can serve two masters: for either he will hate the one, and love the other; or else he will hold to the one, and despise the other. Ye cannot serve God and mammon.

gratification of our material desires that will bring us into full humanity, but the living out of this new kind of life: a heavenly life lived on earth now. It is a richly imaginative life, a life in which the spark of our humanity meets the oil of God's spirit to bring warmth and light to the world.

Jesus expresses the route into this life in terms of two human organs: the heart and the eyes. These two organs and the way we use them contribute more than anything to the life we end up living. The heart speaks essentially of what it is that we want and the eyes of what it is that we watch. Are our hearts set on the new kind of life Jesus offers, or on the quick comforts of the consumer lifestyle? Like an inner compass, our innermost longings set direction for our lives. Do we find our passions and energies, our dreams and desires, drawn towards the justice and mercy of God, or towards our own comfort? Whichever is the case, whichever direction our hearts are set towards, the journey of our life will be affected. And the heart, more often than not, follows the eyes. Making a connection that uncannily predicts the image-centred consumerism that would emerge centuries later, Jesus understands how deeply what we watch impacts on what we want. In a remarkable survey in the America of the late twentieth century, sociologist Juliet Schor found this link to be statistically provable, claiming that 'TV inflates our sense of what's normal.'[80] In one survey, Schor discovered that every hour of television viewed per week raised consumption by an additional $208 per year. Wherever you allow your eye to linger, you can be sure that your willpower and wallet will soon follow.

Get the direction of your heart and eyes wrong, Jesus warns, and you will find that you have a new master. Mammon, the destructive spiritual power behind the craving for wealth, will challenge the very role of God in your life. Unless we focus ourselves toward heaven, the throne of God, we become Mammon's slaves. We pour so much energy into 'owning' the fruits of the earth that we have no strength left to enjoy them.

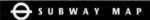

SUBWAY MAP

STATION
Deuteronomy 8:10-20 – the power of wealth and comfort to sap our spiritual strength.

CONNECTIONS
Matthew 19:23, Mark 4:19, 1 Timothy 6:9 – three examples of the battle that rages between material comfort and spiritual growth.

2. HIGH ANXIETY

Location *Matthew 6:25-34.* Therefore I tell you, do not worry about your life, what you will eat or drink; or about your body, what you will wear. Is not life more important than food, and the body more important than clothes? Look at the birds of the air; they do not sow or reap or store away in barns, and yet your heavenly Father feeds them. Are you not much more valuable than they? Who of you by worrying can add a single hour to his life? And why do you worry about clothes? See how the lilies of the field grow. They do not labour or spin. Yet I tell you that not even Solomon in all his splendour was dressed like one of these. If that is how God clothes the grass of the field, which is here today and tomorrow is thrown into the fire, will he not much more clothe you, O you of little faith? So do not worry, saying, 'What shall we eat?' or 'What shall we drink?' or 'What shall we wear?' For the pagans run after all these things, and your heavenly Father knows that you need them. But seek first his kingdom and his righteousness, and all these things will be given to you as well. Therefore do not worry about tomorrow, for tomorrow will worry about itself. Each day has enough trouble of its own."

Landmarks Jesus offers us a straight swap: the heaviness and angst of our worries and anxieties for the lightness and joy of God's provision. We trade our concerns that strangle and destroy us, for the kingdom concerns that bring us life.

What to see A statistician recently reported that eight out of ten people going into a shop to buy a self-help book need help to find it. It was a joke, of course, but an indication also of the fact that the term self-help has now well and truly arrived in our vocabulary. Whether it is through books and seminars, relaxation techniques or self-hypnosis tapes, there has been an explosive market in recent years for pills and products to build self-esteem, overcome fear, tackle pressures and anxieties and usher us into 'successful living'. At the very heart of this market place is a concept that a growing number of people reach for to describe their daily lives: stress. Stress is the new all-encompassing word that brings together the older themes of worry, exhaustion, anxiety and fear, and stress-busting is the new global goal. Whatever our level of business and activity, whatever our field of work, there are very few of us that would claim to lead stress-free lives. And while the language and liturgies with which we list the causes of our stress may be modern and post-modern, the disease itself is ancient. Even in the 'simpler' times into which Jesus spoke, it seems that worry about possessions was a common phenomenon. Then as now, it was a dangerous distraction from the business of the kingdom of God.

Jesus makes two statements about worry. Firstly, he identifies where it comes from. He names food and clothing as the twin engines of anxiety. It was the pursuit of these two commodities, and the fear of their loss that accounted for the anxiety in the lives of those Jesus addressed. And it still does. We have multiplied exponentially the number of ways in which you can worry about food and clothing, and we have added to them a dazzlingly long list of other things to worry about, but at heart the fear of hunger and nakedness remain. It is instructive that the major exhibition centres of the UK report that there are only three types of exhibition that will pull truly massive crowds. The first two are food and clothes shows. The third is the one we have added: transport. Buy any glossy, popular magazine and ask yourself whether food and clothing continue to spark our anxieties.

The second statement that Jesus makes about worry is what to do with it. He offers three cures:

■ **Know your place in the creation**. His reference to sparrows and lilies is deliberately organic. These are two creatures that owe their beauty, inner and outer, and their health not to work and worry, but to the gracious generosity of their Maker. Base your life, Jesus is saying, on the wild, creative kindness of God. Root yourself in him, and find your place in his created world.

■ **Seek the kingdom**. It is remarkable that the very themes that Jesus touches here – of poverty, hunger and nakedness – echo so strongly the Beatitudes. It is our hunger for God that leads to blessing, and our poverty of spirit. We come to God offering nothing and accepting everything. Naked, poor, wretched and blind we come to our Father for mercy. The very feelings that bring us worry can become the passion and fire of our search for God. Don't waste your hunger on food; harness it for the kingdom.

■ **Discipline your thoughts**. The plan is simple: don't waste thoughts on regretting yesterday nor on second-guessing tomorrow – deal with the reality that faces you today. This does not forbid genuine reflection on past experiences, nor consideration of future possibilities, but it does outlaw 'if only' and 'what if?' obsessions. Such obsessions account for a remarkable proportion of the time we invest in worrying, and the only way to deal with them is to kill them dead. Jesus pinpoints the real irony of so much of our worrying that it is so rooted in speculation, fantasy and wild imagining that it can have no positive benefit on the real world.

What to do

Name what's nagging. Write down honestly the things that you find yourself worrying about most. Ask yourself how you might trust them to God. Then write against each one 'yesterday', 'today' or 'tomorrow' to indicate which are rooted in regret, which in real need and which in speculation. Prioritise those marked 'today' and decide what action you are going to take.

Bring what bugs you. Each evening, name the things that are 'on your mind' before God. Not as prayer in which you ask for solutions, but simply to acknowledge that these things have bugged you through the day. Whether you use a written or mental list, make an attempt in prayer to hand these things over to God. If necessary, say "Dear God, you have to be up all night anyway, and there's no point in us both losing sleep, so I'm handing this list over to you."

Pray with persistence. Where you have regular, recurring worries make it a habit to hand them over to God in prayer every time they fight for your attention. Do it over and over again if need be, but always do it before the worries have tempted you into conversation. If necessary say "This file has been transferred, and is no longer in my department. I'm afraid I can't help you." Then slam the enquiry hatch shut.

Places to stay

Anxiety and prayer are more opposed to each other than fire and water.
J.A. Bengel[83]

To discover God in the smallest and most ordinary things, as well as in the greatest, is to possess a rare and sublime faith. To find contentment in the present moment is to relish and adore the divine will in the succession of all things to be done and suffered which make up the duty to the present moment... Nothing is hidden from his eyes. He walks alike over the smallest blade of grass, the tallest cedars, grains of sand or rocky mountains. Wherever you go he has gone before. Only follow him and you will find him everywhere. *Jean-Pierre de Caussade*[84]

R E T R O - T O U R

Therefore I say unto you, Take no thought for your life, what ye shall eat, or what ye shall drink; nor yet for your body, what ye shall put on. Is not the life more than meat, and the body than raiment? Behold the fowls of the air: for they sow not, neither do they reap, nor gather into barns; yet your heavenly Father feedeth them. Are ye not much better than they? Which of you by taking thought can add one cubit unto his stature? And why take ye thought for raiment? Consider the lilies of the field, how they grow; they toil not, neither do they spin: And yet I say unto you, That even Solomon in all his glory was not arrayed like one of these. Wherefore, if God so clothe the grass of the field, which today is, and tomorrow is cast into the oven, shall he not much more clothe you, O ye of little faith? Therefore take no thought, saying, What shall we eat? or, What shall we drink? or, Wherewithal shall we be clothed? (For after all these things do the Gentiles seek:) for your heavenly Father knoweth that ye have need of all these things. But seek ye first the kingdom of God, and his righteousness; and all these things shall be added unto you. Take therefore no thought for the morrow: for the morrow shall take thought for the things of itself. Sufficient unto the day is the evil thereof."

It is fussing about ski boots when you are on your way to the beach. Deal with the day in hand: focus on what faces you.

Against this backdrop of the foolishness and futility of a worry-filled life, Jesus paints an alternative picture. Through this passage, he speaks continually in terms of 'more' and 'all'. Life is more important than clothes; we are more important than the birds; how much more will God clothe us than the grass; when we seek God all these things will be given to us. The intention is clear: it is to lift our eyes from the pettiness of our worries to be caught by a higher vision. The life of simple trust in God is an invitation not to less, but to more: to a life so rich, creative, imaginative and beautiful that we will wonder how we could have worried so much about food. To the young person so driven to 'look good' that eating disorders wreak havoc, Jesus says, 'Look higher, for a deeper beauty'. To the work-stressed employee doing triple shifts just to pay-off the car loan, Jesus says 'Look higher, there is a more satisfying way'. To the family so wrapped up in keeping up with the neighbours that there is no time left for each other, Jesus says 'Look higher, there is a richer life.' The route to a worry-free life does not consist of rejecting beauty, pleasure, colour, creativity and flavour for a bland, tasteless and utilitarian life. It consists of walking in daily trust with the Creator in whom all grace and beauty are founded and dancing with him into a life of higher goals, deeper beauty and more lasting satisfaction.

3. HERE COMES THE JUDGE

Location *Matthew 7:1-6.* Do not judge, or you too will be judged. For in the same way you judge others, you will be judged, and with the measure you use, it will be measured to you. "Why do you look at the speck of sawdust in your brother's eye and pay no attention to the plank in your own eye? How can you say to your brother, 'Let me take the speck out of your eye,' when all the time there is a plank in your own eye? You hypocrite, first take the plank out of your own eye, and then you will see clearly to remove the speck from your brother's eye. Do not give dogs what is sacred; do not throw your pearls to pigs. If you do, they may trample them under their feet, and then turn and tear you to pieces.

Landmarks Let go and let God – how to trust God to deal with others as gently and firmly as he deals with us. Of planks and pettiness – living with a generous spirit. Don't trash God's human jewels!

What to see The most intriguing aspect of Jesus' statements about judgement is just where they sit in Matthew's narrative. Jesus has looked at worry and anxiety and will go on, in the following passage, to describe the life of simple trust in which we ask God for what we need and receive it. The two ideas are closely linked, since worry is the absence of trust and trust is the antidote to worry. But sitting between them, like an interruption to a television drama, is something very different. Here we are talking about how we see others, and the speed with which we rush to correct their faults without even thinking of our own.

If you look deeper there is a close connection. In dealing with worry Jesus has hit on the very heart of the matter: we worry because we are unwilling to trust God to look after us. Afraid that his route to beauty and satisfaction is unreliable or unworkable, we establish short cuts based on our own efforts and energies. And judgement, as it turns out, is the same process turned on others.

In worry, it is our own growth and development we will not leave to God: in judgement it is the growth and development of others. Unwilling to allow God to be sovereign over the lives of those around us, we impose our own sovereignty and standards and insist that they measure up to us. In order to stress the foolishness of such activities, Jesus draws a cartoon. In it a man is trying, with the help of bright lights, tweezers and a magnifying glass, to remove a speck of sawdust from his friend's eye. The problem is he can hardly get close enough because out of his own eye there protrudes a six-foot length of floorboard. The message is simple: not only is he wrong to direct attention to his brother's faults – he is also incapable of doing anything about them.

Judgement is the other half of worry because it lives in the same virtual world,

the unreality of regret, fantasy and speculation. Just as worry contributes nothing to my own growth, so judgement is incapable of helping others to grow. Both are a waste of time and energy. Neither has anything to offer the real needs of a real world. And both grow from the same stubborn root: the refusal to let God be God, and trust him. The solution lies in trust. If I trust God for my own growth, letting him remove the woodwork from my eye, then I will learn to trust him for the growth of others, and may even be in a position to help them. It is those who have undergone the surgery of God who are most fitted to help prospective patients. Those who have never so much as lain on the operating table have nothing to offer.

In our own fast-paced, image-rich age of consumerism, judgement, like worry, has been enshrined in everyday practice. The very foundation of advertising is comparison: the separation of the population into 'winners' and 'losers'. The images and campaigns that fuel our anxieties and drive us to the lap of Mammon are the same images that cause us to judge ourselves and others. Our perceptions are all too full of people who, by our standards, are too fat, too thin, too poor, too rich, too ugly, too noisy, too quiet, too radical, too conservative, too boring or too wild to deserve our love. We blunder plank-eyed into their lives, wondering why they haven't yet asked us for help in sawdust-removal.

What to do

Let go and let God. Reflect on the people around you to whom you have been tempted to offer sawdust-removal services. What might it mean for you to step back, and trust God to be responsible for their growth? How can you redirect the energy you have used to judge them into prayer for God to bless them?

Count the pearls. Reflect on the groups in the wider population that you tend to devalue and dehumanise, those you judge 'losers'. Ask God to transform your heart until you see them as pearls in his creation.

Process the planks. There is a link between sawdust and wood. Very often the things we so mercilessly judge in others point to the very areas in which we need help. Think about the type of sawdust that you find it hardest to tolerate in others, and ask God if you are carrying a plank of the same type.

Places to stay

Petty people are ugly people. They are people who have lost their vision. They are people who have turned their eyes away from what matters and focused, instead, on what doesn't matter. The result is that the rest of us are immobilised by their obsession with the insignificant. ... Petty people are dangerous people because they appear to be only a nuisance instead of what they really are – a health hazard. *Mike Yaconelli*[85]

When our minds, hearts and imaginations are no longer poised for surprise and astonishment, when we feel we have already understood something, then we no longer have a healthy fear of God, nor indeed of each other. *Ronald Rolheiser*[86]

R E T R O - T O U R

Judge not, that ye be not judged. For with what judgement ye judge, ye shall be judged: and with what measure ye mete, it shall be measured to you again. And why beholdest thou the mote that is in thy brother's eye, but considerest not the beam that is in thine own eye? Or how wilt thou say to thy brother, Let me pull out the mote out of thine eye; and, behold, a beam is in thine own eye? Thou hypocrite, first cast out the beam out of thine own eye; and then shalt thou see clearly to cast out the mote out of thy brother's eye. Give not that which is holy unto the dogs, neither cast ye your pearls before swine, lest they trample them under their feet, and turn again and rend you.

DISTRICT 4: FINANCIAL

Think again, Jesus says. Treating people in this way is like taking precious jewels and throwing them to a herd of pigs. It is like taking the best and richest of food, beautifully prepared, and throwing it out the window for the street dogs to eat. This image recurs in Acts 10, in a vision in which Peter is instructed 'Do not call anything impure that God has made clean.' There as here, the image is of food, but it is people God is talking about. Know the true value of things, and the true value of people. Human beings are the image-bearers of God; they are his jewels. Don't treat them as garbage.

 S U B W A Y   M A P

STATION
Psalm 7:1-17 – it is God's prerogative to judge, and we can trust him to do it well.

CONNECTIONS
Romans 14:4, Romans 14:13, I Corinthians 4:5, James 4:12 – the banning of judgmentalism from the New Testament church.

---

4. KNOCK, KNOCK, WHOSE HEIR?

Location *Matthew 7:7-12.* Ask and it will be given to you; seek and you will find; knock and the door will be opened to you. For everyone who asks receives; he who seeks finds; and to him who knocks, the door will be opened. Which of you, if his son asks for bread, will give him a stone? Or if he asks for a fish, will give him

a snake? If you, then, though you are evil, know how to give good gifts to your children, how much more will your Father in heaven give good gifts to those who ask him! So in everything, do to others what you would have them do to you, for this sums up the Law and the Prophets.

Landmarks There is no substitute for an interactive relationship with a loving parent, and no better image of the love of God for us.

What to see In all the discussion of both worry and judgement, Jesus has been hinting at the central place of trust to our faith: and here he makes the hint explicit. The alternative to a life of anxiety in which we are consumed with fears of hunger and nakedness – and likewise the alternative to a life of judgement in which we lunge at sawdust with planks – is a relationship of trust with our Creator. In both cases, the negative emotion is replaced not by dull neutrality but by a positive relationship. The opposite of worry is not the absence of worry, but the presence of God. The opposite of judgement is not neutrality but love. In all these matters, at the heart of our relationships with the human and non-human creation, there is the abiding, central need for a relationship with our Father.

The language Jesus uses here is very precise. The danger of the 'ask and you will receive' promise is that God becomes a cosmic vending machine. We simply

What to do

Think about what you might do to rekindle relationship with a perfect parent you hadn't seen for a while. You might want to take the time to visit; to write a letter; to take a walk together. Whatever it is you would do – do the same in your relationship with God.

Make a list of the things you have asked God for in recent weeks. Reflect on which of these you asked for as you might ask a loving parent, and which belong more to the divine vending machine model. Keep the first list; throw away the second.

Make another list, this time of all the things you can name that are evidence, in your life, of the grace and generosity of God. Take some time out to say thank you.

drop the coinage of our desires into the appropriate slot and wait for his provision to be delivered. It is this 'automatic response' interpretation that has fuelled, over the centuries, the tendency towards a 'health and wealth' gospel. Jesus heads off this interpretation by moving swiftly into the language of family and fatherhood. Our relationship with the Creator is not one of clients or customers, nor are we entitled to expect magic responses to our needs: it is the relationship of growing children to their perfect parent. At the heart of every transaction there is this dynamic, two-way conversation. No gift is given without the whispered 'I love you' and the glint in the eye that says 'this is from me'. And behind every gift is the commitment to our health and growth: a commitment deeper than our own to our best interests.

We ask, seek, knock not because we have a magic formula by which God can be forced to bless us, but because we have a loving parent who wants the very best for us. The writer Adrian Plass once wrote that it was only after he had been a Christian for several years that he discovered the one truth that really matters, 'God is nice and he likes me.' The same truth is the treasure at the heart of these words of Jesus.

To attempt to build such a relationship without engaging the giver in conversation, without inviting him to advise us on just what we should ask for, is the highest foolishness. As it turns out, many mature disciples discover that God's advice is the greatest of his gifts: that the direction he brings to our lives outweighs by far the benefits we might have received from the 'things' we thought we wanted.

DISTRICT 4: FINANCIAL

The wonder of God is not only that he won't give you stones when you ask for bread, but that he won't even give you stones when you ask for stones.

It is only by placing this relational dynamic at the heart of the teachings of Jesus that we will avoid the extremes and misinterpretations many have known. God longs to bless you, but over and above that, he longs to know you. Like the parent who provides for his children, he wants to be more than a paymaster, taxi driver, cook and launderer: he wants our love.

Almost as an afterthought, the words widely known as The Golden Rule, summarised in oral culture as 'do as you would be done by' are slipped into the end of this discourse. The generosity of God is not only to be the basis on which we build our relationship with him, and

Places to stay

When I bow before his love he is not slow to come; rather he has already come, for he loves me much more than I, poor creature, can ever love him. And love shows itself in action, as for the Prodigal Son. Rising up is a fact, leaving the pigs is a fact. The soul must say with sincerity, 'Now I will arise and go to my Father.' *Carlo Carretto*[87]

Happiness of heart can no more be obtained without God than light and sunshine can be had without the sun. Happiness is heavenly born; its aroma is of heaven; it leads to heaven and its emblem is heaven. On every side, in every part of the universe men and women are seeking happiness and cannot find it because they do not seek it from God. *Father Bernard Vaughan*[88]

R E T R O · T O U R

Ask, and it shall be given you; seek, and ye shall find; knock, and it shall be opened unto you: For every one that asketh receiveth; and he that seeketh findeth; and to him that knocketh it shall be opened. Or what man is there of you, whom if his son ask bread, will he give him a stone? Or if he ask a fish, will he give him a serpent? If ye then, being evil, know how to give good gifts unto your children, how much more shall your Father which is in heaven give good things to them that ask him? Therefore all things whatsoever ye would that men should do to you, do ye even so to them: for this is the law and the prophets.

grow in trust: it is also to be the basis on which we treat others. The greatest tragedy in humanity is to see someone who has received abundantly from the generous, non-judging mercy of God, and yet cannot extend the same grace to those around. It is in the relationship of simple trust of God that the love of our neighbour becomes possible, viable, fruitful and real. The Golden Rule, without the perfect parent, is an empty promise.

 **SUBWAY MAP**

STATION
Deuteronomy 32:1-6 – Moses' song of the fatherhood and faithfulness of God.

CONNECTIONS
Revelation 3:14-22 – we knock on God's door but sometimes he knocks on ours!

---

5. LIMITED LUGGAGE ALLOWANCE

Location *Matthew 7:13-14*. Enter through the narrow gate. For wide is the gate and broad is the road that leads to destruction, and many enter through it. But small is the gate and narrow the road that leads to life, and only a few find it.

Landmarks One carry-on bag only: squeezing through the narrowest of gates. Engine failure; taking the long route home.

What to see Visit the check-in desks of most airlines – particularly those operating short-haul flights – and it won't be long before you witness a certain scene. A passenger, checking-in, will be insistent that their bag should qualify as carry-on baggage. A harassed assistant will be trying hard to tell them otherwise. Some airlines have become so frustrated with the constant arguments that they now have a metal frame available alongside the desk that mimics the exact dimensions of a luggage locker. If you can't squeeze your bag into the frame, you won't be able to squeeze it into the locker.

This captures something of the picture that Jesus is using here, of a gate so narrow that you can barely squeeze yourself through it, let alone your worldly goods. There is a well-known image which Jesus uses elsewhere to describe the struggle of getting a rich man into God's kingdom: the image of a camel passing through the eye of a needle.[89] Some scholars claim that this is essentially the same concept as the narrow gate mentioned here. They suspect that one of the Jerusalem city gates may have been called 'the needle's eye', and was so small as to be reserved for pedestrian use only: a merchant trying to get through it with a heavily-laden camel would soon find himself stuck tight. Picture the driver of a high vehicle realising, too late, that he has just tried to get under a low bridge, and you get the same image. It may just be that the things we cling to, the wealth and comforts we have accumulated, the strengths and sufficiencies we rely on to get us through every barrier will all have to be dropped as we pass into the kingdom of God. It is not because these things are bad in themselves, but because we must come poor and naked, dependent only on the love and mercy of God. God loves us for who we are, not for who we project ourselves to be.

Beyond the wide and small gates are two roads, once more characterised as broad and narrow. The broad road is the easiest to find and follow. It is the way of the crowd. The narrow road is harder to discern, and is the road less travelled. The image does not imply that the way of Christ is all misery and woe: a steep climb up a rocky road with little comfort or

What to do

Check what you're carrying. What baggage do you carry with you that you might find hard to bring into God's kingdom? Are there possessions you are afraid to lose, or grudges you won't drop? Is your relationship with God unconditional – or do you secretly say 'this far and no further'? If you are carrying excess baggage, hand it over now to God.

Take the high road. Are there areas of your life in which you always take short-cuts, refusing to operate at God's slower, more measured pace? Give these areas to him and ask him for new routes.

Look for signs of life. Consider your journey with God of recent months. What were the roadside signs by which he has spoken to you? Did you stop to reflect, or rush on by? Thank him for the signs of his presence, and take time now to reflect and consider.

When I am tempted to rush from A to B with neither reflection nor thought – help me Lord to take the road less travelled.

When I am caught up with the crowd, drawn to the easy way but knowing I should take another route – help me Lord to take the road less travelled.

When my luggage weighs me down, and I carry so much with me that I can barely make the climb – help me Lord to set non-essentials aside, and take the road less travelled.

compensation. But it does imply that there is work involved. To take the obvious route, to follow the first option offered, is to move with the crowd on a path that has no promise of life. The way of Jesus is reflective and thoughtful. It is imaginative and creative, and takes time to find and master. Our tendency to take the easy option is demonstrated in our own era by our driving habits. How many of us, given the need to drive from London to Birmingham, will choose the stop-start, winding traffic of B roads, when the motorways are available to us? We want to get where we're going, and get there fast. But the road to life, Jesus tells us, doesn't work like that. It is a slow road, measured in its pace. It features stops along the way; detours and diversions. There are people to talk to as we travel, and sites to see. If we are unwilling to slow down, and even at times to stop, we will never see the many wonders of the world God has made. He puts flowers in the hedgerows for our pleasure: but we fly past them in a blur.

The narrow road is the road of human frailty, of travel unassisted by jet engines. It is the road of gentle conversation, on which the whisper of God is not drowned-out by a million motors. It is a road on which we have time for people, time for reflection and growth, time for our

Places to stay

Nobody climbs a mountain pulling a trailer behind them. To move on and up in Godzone, you have to learn to let go... To grasp, to cling, to hold on, these come naturally. To let go without being forced to is to share in the life of God. *Mike Riddell*[90]

'No-landers' are looking collectively for a Kingdom of Heaven through the dark windows of their mortality. But the Kingdom of Heaven is a country which can only be seen by the light of the spirit which shines in each soul. If we set out for it alone we shall reach it together. *Kitty Muggeridge*[91]

R E T R O - T O U R

Enter ye in at the strait gate: for wide is the gate, and broad is the way, that leadeth to destruction, and many there be which go in thereat: Because strait is the gate, and narrow is the way, which leadeth unto life, and few there be that find it.

relationship with the Creator. For some of us, it is a road we can only reach by turning off our present route.

There is an interesting double-meaning to end this image. This narrow road, this slower, gentler, more subtle way of living will, according to Jesus, 'lead to life'. This means two things at once. In one sense, it means what Christians have always taken it

to mean, that following the way of Christ will take us to the final destination of eternal life in God. But it also means something else: that as we travel this road, as we slow our pace, and stop to reflect, and make time for people, and seek depth in our lives, then we will discover in the midst of our journey that we are truly alive. Life is found not only at the end of this road but also on the road itself.

Tourist information Panel

TIP 7 – Local Politics

Palestine was a dangerous place to be at the time of Jesus. From the hills around Galilee, gangs of armed militiamen would sweep down and raid the granaries and storehouses of the rich. These militia, or groups of bandits, had often lost their land to the wealthy – forced into debt, they mortgaged their land and when they could not repay the debt, the land was confiscated. Of course, the Jubilee laws had decreed that the land should be given back to its rightful owner but that never seemed to have happened. Instead, the rich got richer and the poor starved to death.

Palestine, and especially Upper Galilee was a poor place with a 50 per cent infant mortality rate due to starvation alone. Most people eked out a living on the land through subsistence agriculture. Sometimes they could

supplement their diet with gleanings from hillside plants, sometimes from the Sea of Galilee and its rich fishing stock. But the Sea, and all that was in it, was actually the property of the King. Fishing was heavily taxed and even those who could set up a small co-operative industry like Zebedee and his sons were still on subsistence level incomes because of this punitive taxation.

Remember Levi and Zacchaeus, the tax collectors? The local political rulers franchised out their tax raising – a bit like privatising the Inland Revenue. As long as they got their tax, the tax collector could add on his own administrative costs as appropriate. All that mattered was that the King had his share. Taxes were everywhere, from the countryside to the Temple in Jerusalem.

Of course, the rich were fabulously rich, especially the Jerusalem aristocracy, often associated with the Temple priesthood and the group we know as Sadduccees. The royal dynasty of Herod's three sons, Antipas, Archelaus and Philip owned vast tracks of fertile land in the Jordan valley. The land was apportioned to each of them. Antipas looked after Galilee and the area across the Jordan called the Decapolis. As a good Roman puppet-king, he built splendid new Roman cities at Sepphoris (about four miles from Nazareth) and Tiberias on the Sea of Galilee. Philip gained the north east and he too set to building new cities, especially Bethsaida, the home of Peter, Andrew and Philip. Archelaus ruled Judea for a decade before being overthrown by Rome. In his place they established a minor civil servant post of the Procurator. Pilate and Felix held this office during different times in the New Testament story.

Poverty of the masses and the wealth of the minority: this sums up the social scene of Jesus' day. At the pinnacle of the wealth pyramid was the Emperor, figurehead of the Roman state and the power that let Herod's family continue to rule, at least in Galilee and the north for much of the first century.

TIP 8 – Local Factions

Central to Judaism were the two strands of ritual and lifestyle, halakah

and haggadah. T[...]
around these the[...]
and the Pharise[...]

The Sadduccees were [...]
Jerusalem and the priesthood. The[...]
represented the vested interests of the Temple and sought renewal for Judaism through the Temple ritual, through doing things in the proper way and by maintaining tradition.

The Pharisees, on the other hand, saw revival as coming through a proper interpretation of God's law – through lives lived according to God's ways. Holiness was central to the Pharisees. Rather than centre their work around the Temple, the Pharisees were scattered throughout the communities of Palestine. They would normally have an occupation, often as a day labourer, artisan or farmer. After doing their work, they would talk with villagers and often had a group of disciples learning from them. Much of this discipleship involved learning the first five books of the Old Testament.

The Essenes were a small group of devotees to holiness. They lived both in desert communities in the Jordan valley (Qumran is the most famous) as well as in some of the major cities. They thought that the Sadduccees and Pharisees had polluted Temple worship and destroyed true Judaism. As such

withdraw from society and
ocused on purification and holiness.
They saw themselves as soldiers of the
light, fighting alongside the Spirit and
angels of light against the forces of
darkness. They fervently studied
scripture and venerated Moses. Most of
the Essenes were killed when they took
on the Romans, the forces of darkness,
during the Jewish uprisings.

Most people in Palestine were not
members of any of these groups. They
were the normal people, the people of
the land. They sought to follow God's
ways and the ways that they had been
taught in their communities. Central to
them were concepts of kinship, loyalty,
honour and steadfast love, the central
concepts of God's covenant love
shown through their history as a Jewish
people. Judaism and its new offshoot
Christianity offered them a new kinship
with God and his people – 'Anyone
who does the will of my Father is my
brother and sister and mother.'
(Matthew 12:50)

DISTRICT 5: FRUITFUL
The Artisan Quarter
Matthew 7:15 - 7:29

Orientation and information

Within the confines of many modern cities there will be a district known as the old city. Whether this is in fact the oldest part of town is academic: it will be the district in which the activities of the city are deemed to have been conducted over the longest time period. In some cases it will be an area still marked out by the ancient walls that were once the city's edge. In the European context, this will often be a place of cobbled streets and alleyways, with small shops and businesses squeezed into the cramped quarters of buildings designed for a pre-consumer age. In many cities this will be the artisans' quarter, a gathering place for artists and craftspeople of every kind. In others still it will be a collectors' area, weighed down with new and second-hand goods – from faded postage stamps to paintings and pottery fresh from the studio kiln. In most cases, the maze of narrow alleys will open up at the heart of the district onto a market square. This will be a place that was once the hub of everyday life but has become, in an age of city-edge hypermarkets and malls, more a centre for tourism and leisure.

Scattered across the uneven cobbles of the square will be the stalls of an eclectic mix of merchants, market gardeners and master craftsmen. There are fruits and cheeses, breads and cured meats. There is glassware, brassware, tableware and copperware. Here is a table so weighed down with books that it sags like a tired old dog. There is a shoe stall, itself ankle deep in slippers and trainers. In the Market Square of Prague you can see medals manufactured as they were four hundred years ago, and buy the results. In Vienna you can taste the warm gluhwein without which a central European Christmas is not complete. In London, so the song tells us, 'anything and everything a chap can unload can be bought off a barrow in the Portobello Road.'

The scene is noisy and colourful, bustling with life. What is true of the cobbled alleys and shop-lined streets is also true of the crowded market: the goods on display are in some measure the fruits of the labour and investment of their sellers. There is hard work involved; long hours and at times physical exhaustion. There is passion and commitment to a cause. The cucumber you buy has been planted, nurtured and harvested by the old woman you buy it from. The salamis hung from the roof bars have been cured by the family busy underneath them. The bright paintings that catch your eye as you pass represent hours of painstaking work by the young woman who sits sketching beside the display. Whether the effort of those present has gone into locating merchandise and preparing it for sale, into choosing and displaying stock, or into creating works and wares from nothing, there is care and love and longevity in their work.

There is something in the long-haul lifestyle of artists, artisans and craftspeople that resonates with the life Jesus seems to be describing in this final section of the Sermon on the Mount. He steers deliberately away from religious performance and quick-fix solutions to speak of a deeper life, a life lived in the long-term. There is care and investment needed in building for strength, on the right foundations. Above all there is fruit borne over years in our lives.

The invitation to follow Jesus is not an easy option – here Jesus makes it so difficult as to appear almost obstructive. It is an invitation to engage in personal change and to retrain for the craft of fruit-bearing. At the heart of the adventure is the knowledge and acceptance of the will of God. This miracle – the opportunity to know and fulfil the purposes of the Creator – is accessed by those prepared

for hard work, those who are not put off when roads become mountainous and the harvest is long in coming. In order to find such people, Jesus must put off those in search of easy experience. Having lowered the bar in the Beatitudes so that even the poorest of the poor can come in, he now raises the standard so that only those serious about a new kind of life will want to. The images are harsh and the talk tough, showing us that the stakes are high. It is the kind of life we want to lead that hangs in the balance here. Will we choose the soft option of going with the crowd and adding a religious veneer for effect, or will we take the road less travelled – to a kingdom kind a life: a future life lived in the now? The only place success comes before work is in the dictionary.

HIGHLIGHTS

- Skin-deep beauty or deeply fruity?
- Flushing out false followers
- Of bodgers and builders
- The common touch

1. SKIN-DEEP BEAUTY OR DEEPLY FRUITY?

Location *Matthew 7:15-20*. Watch out for false prophets. They come to you in sheep's clothing, but inwardly they are ferocious wolves. By their fruit you will recognise them. Do people pick grapes from thorn bushes, or figs from thistles? Likewise every good tree bears good fruit, but a bad tree bears bad fruit. A good tree cannot bear bad fruit, and a bad tree cannot bear good fruit. Every tree that does not bear good fruit is cut down and thrown into the fire. Thus, by their fruit you will recognise them.

Landmarks Don't let appearances fool you, let God deal with the depths of you. Find fruitfulness in the unforced rhythms of grace.

What to See Fake Rolex watches look great when you first buy them. Laid out on a market table, they have the same glitz and glamour of the real thing, at a fraction of the cost. In the first few days of their life, you can even reproduce the classic Rolex trick of submerging them, without harm, in a pint of beer. It is over time, as they receive the knocks of daily wear and are put to use in the real world, that the gilt starts to fade and they are shown for what they are. It is one thing to reproduce the outward appearance of a great watch, but quite another to have the real deal on the inside. There are many similar examples of goods that look their best at the point of sale, but don't

stand up to the test of time. This is the kind of thinking that Jesus applies to the sphere of spirituality. He makes a stark distinction, often forgotten by the Jews of his day, between the outward appearance of piety and the inner reality of faith. Because the two look so similar, it is only long-term fruitfulness that will separate them. The only way to distinguish the real from the fake is to test it out on the hard terrain of everyday life: and the most essential factor in the test is time.

I have a friend in West Africa who applies this concept quite literally to the calling of new church leaders. Responsible on behalf of his denomination for a large geographical area, he is constantly presented with young people convinced that God has called them to plant churches. His method of selection is simple: each person sensing this call is taken to an area where there is no church, and left for one year. 'If there is a church after one year', my friend explains, 'we say that they are called to plant churches. If there is nothing, we suggest they find another job.' The approach is not intended simply to reward success or to mark out winners from losers. Rather, it is a radical application of this biblical principle, that it is only by fruitfulness that a true calling can be identified.

All the vision and bluster in the world cannot produce so much as a pip – and all the self doubt in the world cannot reduce the miracle of an apple. Jesus appeals to thorns and figs to prove his case because

DISTRICT 5: FRUITFUL

he is talking about principles that are written into the very fabric of the universe. The fruit of a tree or bush will tell you almost everything you need to know about the tree: what it is, what genetic family it belongs to, whether it is in a healthy or unhealthy state. Fruitfulness is not a metaphor for the way life works, it is the way life works. It is well worth taking time to draw out the principles wrapped up in this focus on fruitfulness, in order that we might set realistic targets for our lives.

■ **Fruit is seasonal**. There is a rhythm to fruitfulness – times of planting, of cutting back; times of nurture and waiting; times of harvest. It is said of olive groves that it takes from eight to ten years to bring a newly planted grove to the beginnings of real fruitfulness. A similar period is needed to get the best from a vineyard: the 'fruity' image that Jesus refers to most often. Two things can be said of this approach in our own day. The first is that we talk as if we know this to be true. The second is that we live as if it isn't. We say that we are not fooled by appearances but time and again we give accolades to the apparently fabulous while the truly fruitful go unnoticed. Our use of the media as the appropriate means of identifying our heroes leads inevitably to a short-term perspective and to an overemphasis on the immediacy of glamour. Success we understand – but fruitfulness is another ball game altogether.

■ **Fruit grows from inner health**. Fruit farmers really have little concern for the outward appearance of the trees they care for, except where appearance tells them something about inner health. It is the internal strength and health of the tree that dictates the sweetness of its fruit. It is all too easy for us to judge our lives, and those of others, on the basis of appearances, and to miss the real beauty that is fruitfulness. One of the ways in which we often misunderstand the work of God in our lives is that we ask Him to help us change outwardly, whilst he is committed to our inner transformation. Inner health and long-term fruitfulness are his goals for us: the short-term outward appearance of our lives is a distraction.

■ **Fruit is delivered, not described**. Fruitfulness is not about what we project; or hope for, or are looking forward to, or have vision and faith for: it is about what actually grows. Too often we assess our own progress on the basis of our intentions and potential. This is the equivalent of an apple tree hung with little labels describing good apples – the labels may be eloquent and inspiring, but they are not fruit. Real fruit comes only when intentions are acted on and potential is realised. Some of the most fruitful followers of Jesus are to be found amongst those who say the least but live the most.

■ **You can't argue with fruit**. The surest way to know that the tree you are looking at is an apple tree is to taste the apples hanging from it. Fruit is the final, non-negotiable identifier for the tree or

---

bush on which it grows. Those who love to parade their religion around and who want to be 'known' as God's favourites may look good in the short-term: but if there is no depth to their walk with God this will soon become apparent, when they are the only naked tree in the orchard.

It could be tempting to build, from these few comments, a performance-related picture of what Jesus is saying. Only those disciples who produce results are welcome, it seems. But to take this route is to oversimplify the nature of fruit in our lives. The fruit Jesus is describing does not consist of the 'results' of our various Christian projects: it is something much deeper. It is about conformity to the will of God, about the renewal of our minds and the transformation of our lives. Every moment the prayer 'your will be done' is prayed, even in some small way, there is the possibility of fruitfulness. There is an overlap between fruitfulness and results: but they are not, in essence, the same things.

This section of the Sermon on the Mount is presented as a series of choices. The choice here is between the quick-fix spirituality that makes things look good on the surface and the deeper, long-term investment in inner health. Religion, all too often, takes the first option. True discipleship is measured by its capacity to take the second.

What to do

Focus on fruit. Take a piece of fruit – an apple or orange is ideal. Cut it into halves or quarters. Look closely at its structure, and ask yourself how long it has taken to grow. What nutrients have been patiently invested to produce this goodness? What is God doing in your life that has the equivalent effect of producing hard-won, long-term fruit?

Think about time. Examine the timescale on which you are asking God to work in your life. Are you expecting him to provide quick fixes, a fast lane route to holiness: or are you engaged in the long-term partnership of a fruitful life? If you are in the wrong lane, make plans to shift your expectations.

Deal with depth. Reflect on the extent to which you have invited God to work on the surface of your life, rather than work on your inner health. What are the deeper issues, the ingrained habits and assumptions that get in the way of your long-term health? Invite God, once again, to lead you into dealing with these issues.

DISTRICT 5: FRUITFUL

Places to stay

It is often the small and unexpected things which have greatest impact and the huge, and often expensive, strategic initiative which dies whimpering on the side... Deeds done unnoticed, feelings responded to alone and losses suffered repeatedly are the environment of vision. *Viv Thomas*[92]

The path of spiritual progress is essentially ordinary. It is not outside the path of normality, but in it. It is simply a case of natural growth in what God intends for us all, requiring the immediate contact with him which is the listening responsiveness of contemplative prayer... *Mother Mary Clare SLG*[93]

R E T R O · T O U R

Beware of false prophets, which come to you in sheep's clothing, but inwardly they are ravening wolves. Ye shall know them by their fruits. Do men gather grapes of thorns, or figs of thistles? Even so every good tree bringeth forth good fruit; but a corrupt tree bringeth forth evil fruit. A good tree cannot bring forth evil fruit, neither can a corrupt tree bring forth good fruit. Every tree that bringeth not forth good fruit is hewn down, and cast into the fire. Wherefore by their fruits ye shall know them.

SUBWAY MAP

STATION
Isaiah 5:1-7 – God the organic farmer nurtures his people in the hope that their lives will bear fruit.

CONNECTIONS
John 15:1-17 – Jesus as the vine in whom life, growth and fruitfulness are found.

2. FLUSHING OUT FALSE FOLLOWERS

Location *Matthew 7:21-23*. Not everyone who says to me, 'Lord, Lord,' will enter the kingdom of heaven, but only he who does the will of my Father who is in heaven. Many will say to me on that day, 'Lord, Lord, did we not prophesy in your name, and in your name drive out demons and perform many miracles?' Then I will tell them plainly, 'I never knew you. Away from me, you evildoers!

Landmarks Rhetoric or reality: getting beyond words to the real journey of faith. Putting off the thrill seekers – why Jesus makes it hard to follow him.

What to see It is traditional to see the Pharisees and teachers of the law as the butt of Jesus' humour and the enemy of his words. There is evidence to support this view: it is the hypocrisy of the religious leaders of his day that most offends Jesus and stirs him to anger. The temptation would be to project this view onto Jesus' words about fruitfulness – to see the Pharisees as the impressive but fruitless tree and the followers of Christ as those who bear good fruit. In simplified historical terms, this means seeing Judaism as the faith of empty legalism and Christianity as the faith of loving grace.

But the truth is never so simple. Jesus knows human nature, and he knows that the issues of performance religion are not faced by the Jews alone. He knows that the cause of hypocrisy is not a fault in a particular belief system so much as a fault-line running through the human heart. Every faith movement, even a radical new sect founded by the Son of God himself, is subject to the same temptations. So Jesus turns the spotlight away from the much maligned Jewish leaders, and onto his own followers.

'Even when you have chosen to follow me', he implies, 'even when you have left empty ritual behind and accepted me as your Lord – hypocrisy remains a possibility.' A religious inclination devoid of intentional faith can surface in any heart in any place and time. The only solution is to seek and do the will of God: to take action in response to his command.

It is as if Jesus is heading off, at the outset of the new Christian faith adventure, the very possibility of hijack by religious performers. Like a recruitment advertisement over-stamped with 'Previous applicants need not reapply', Jesus is sending a coded message to those who find their security in religious exuberance but resist personal change. He wants those who follow him to do so for the right reasons. The harshness of the language – with God rejecting even those who have chosen to follow him – is offset by the tense in which the warning is given. This is revealed by the context of the Sermon itself, which takes place early in the ministry of Jesus. At this stage, only a few people – more friends than followers – have made the choice to identify themselves with Jesus. Even amongst them, there is evidence that their own choice is still embryonic. It is arguable from the details given in the Gospels of the faith journey of Peter – a key disciple if ever there was one – that it is only towards the end of Jesus' ministry that he truly begins to understand who Jesus is and what it will mean to follow him. Some would argue that it takes the death and resurrection of Christ to clarify Peter's choice. The followers, then, to whom Jesus is speaking are future followers. He is not bringing the sharp knife of clinical judgement to his existing followers, separating the genuine from the freeloaders, so much as informing those who might consider following him of the true nature of that choice and the costs they will incur in making it. This is Jesus the evangelist, setting out in no uncertain terms the seriousness of the invitation he is making. 'Don't claim me as your Lord', he is saying, 'unless you are prepared to embark on an adventure of change. Don't adopt me as a flavour-of-the-month religious icon: take me on as your partner in the deep journey of faith.' There is an important model here of evangelism that lays out up-front the costs of discipleship: and an implicit rejection of an 'easy-believism' that hides those costs until later.

The warning has a number of important implications.

■ It is not enough to call Jesus 'Lord'. Words alone, no matter how worthy and worshipful, do not make for a life of discipleship. Words may be the beginning – and there is no implication that those who follow Christ should not call him Lord – but to words must be added genuine intention and action. Finding and doing the will of God is the substance from which the Christian life is woven.

What to do

Weigh your words. Reflect on the number of times in the past month you have called Jesus Lord – whether in private prayer, in public worship or in conversation with others. Now consider how many times your actions have confirmed your words, and how often they have contradicted them.

Check your conformity. What are the areas of your life in which you are more conformed to the will of God now than you were, say, twelve months ago? What are the areas in which little progress has been made? Bring these areas to God and ask what steps you might take in the coming weeks to kick-start your conformity to His will.

Get to know Jesus. Take time out to deepen your knowledge of Jesus. Explore his life; reflect on his words. Hold him up before your imagination as the model of humanity towards which God is calling you. Where you see a shortfall in your own behaviour, don't be condemned by it, but make it your goal, with God's help, to move beyond it.

Lord, before I claim to follow you, help me to get to know you. Before I loosely act in your name, help me to better understand your character. Before I give myself the label 'Christian', may I be deserving of the label 'Christlike'.

■ Apparent miracles are no proof of piety. Welcome as they may be, miracles do not prove the righteousness of those who pray for them. This lesson has been learned many times in the history of the Church, not least in the twentieth century. There is a deep mystery here as to why God would answer the prayers of those whose lives displease him: but Jesus is in no doubt that the true test of faith does not lie in miracles but in conformity to the will of God.

■ To truly follow Jesus, you have to get to know him. This principle is implied rather than stated, but the implication is strong. Without knowing the will of God in a given situation, it is impossible to fulfil it, and such knowledge can only come through a depth of relationship. Jesus demonstrated in his own spirituality that it was the intimacy of his relationship with the Father that gave rise to the certainty of his will.

■ We act with Jesus, not simply in his name. There may be a subtle rejection here of those who want to 'use' the name of Jesus without including him in the partnership. This was the case of the seven 'Sons of Sceva', whose ministry came to a violent end in Acts 19.[94] There is power in the name of Jesus, but only to the extent that it remains attached to the person of Jesus.

Places to stay

There are those who know Godzone and those who know about Godzone. Those who know about it know nothing. That does not stop them explaining it to all who will listen. They make faith into a structure called religion, and then climb inside to hide from God. *Mike Riddell*[95]

The challenge in a post-modern world is to be the presence of a transcendent reality here on earth, the embodied community that draws others to Christ through participation in his incarnate presence, the church. *Robert Webber*[96]

R E T R O - T O U R

Not every one that saith unto me, Lord, Lord, shall enter into the kingdom of heaven; but he that doeth the will of my Father which is in heaven. Many will say to me in that day, Lord, Lord, have we not prophesied in thy name? and in thy name have cast out devils? and in thy name done many wonderful works? And then will I profess unto them, I never knew you: depart from me, ye that work iniquity.

DISTRICT 5: FRUITFUL

If the first choice Jesus sets out is between outward appearances and inward health and fruitfulness, this second choice is between an easy gospel of words and a hard life of personal change and challenge. This is a timeless choice, as relevant to the massed Christian churches of late modernity as it was to the straggling few who heard these words for the first time.

 **S U B W A Y   M A P**

STATION
Samuel 15:22, Psalm 51:16-17, Proverbs 26:23, Isaiah 29:13, Ezekiel 33:31-32, Amos 5:21-24 – the longing of God is not for empty words of worship but full lives of compassion.

CONNECTIONS
Matthew 25:31-46 – the basis on which God will judge each one of us.

3. OF BODGERS AND BUILDERS

Location *Matthew 7:24-27. Therefore everyone who hears these words of mine and puts them into practice is like a wise man who built his house on the rock. The rain came down, the streams rose, and the winds blew and beat against that house; yet it did not fall, because it had its foundation on the rock. But everyone who hears these words of mine and does not put them into practice is like a foolish man who built his house on sand. The rain* came down, the streams rose, and the winds blew and beat against that house, and it fell with a great crash.

Landmarks Surviving the great crash: how to build strongly by starting with the right cornerstone. Seeking shalom: Jesus' manifesto for the renewal of humanity.

What to See If ever Jesus used an image the lends itself to physical representation, this was it. Children's songs, action songs, dances and sketches have been inspired for generations by the sheer drama of the falling masonry and sinking sands. The picture is graphic, comic, immediate and compelling – and doubly powerful in a culture in which the majority of homes were self-build projects. The choice offered is personified in two builders; a prophetic precursor of our own culture's Three Little Pigs. It is not difficult to imagine Jesus, the great storyteller, adding drama to his words by his own movements and voice: the 'great crash' of the story's climax ringing out across the hushed crowd. Providing the last word of the great Sermon, the story leaves its listeners with a final, decisive metaphor for the choice that faces each of them: to treat the words of Jesus as mere religious entertainment, or to take them as the bricks and mortar from which a truly worthwhile life might be constructed.

Thus we come full circle to the invitation with which the great Sermon began, to enter in, with God's help, to the fullness of our humanity: to a life of mercy, compassion and joy lived in the grace and wonder of our Creator's friendship.

The household is the heart of all life to the Jewish mind. The relationships formed within it, the activities centred on it, the hours that pass beneath its roof – these are the stuff and substance of our lives. In a culture in which little leisure activity existed outside the home, in which few people travelled and in which most employment was to some degree home-based, the house that a man might choose to build would be the focus of his dreams and aspirations. This truly is a metaphor for the whole breadth of our lives, for everything we love and long for. For the majority of Jesus' listeners, the bricks and mortar of the home were the only property they could ever aspire to own. Wise choices about what to build, where to build and how to build were essential, as Jesus the carpenter would know only too well.

There is a hidden tragedy in this story surrounding the people Jesus doesn't mention: the family of the inept and foolish builder. His concentration in this story on men is not sexism, but a reflection of the culture of the day – and a very important challenge. In Jewish culture it was men who would, on behalf of their family, build the home. It was a rare man who would build for himself alone. The choice to build was a significant moment in a man's life. If the Bar Mitzvah was the signal that a boy had joined the adult male world, the building of a home was the signal that he was ready to marry, raise children and take up his responsibilities in the community. His wife and children would be dependent for their safety and security on his skills and wisdom. For many in the crowd, the first instinct at the sound of 'the great crash' would be to feel pity for the foolish builder's dependants. How sad for a woman to be saddled with such a husband and for a child to have such a man as a father. Our own situation is different, with many households dependent not on the father but on the mother. At a moment early in 2001, American society will pass the point at which over one third of all births are to single mothers, and European culture is not far behind. There is wisdom here for women as well as men. Our response to this story in post-modern times might be to reflect on just who, beyond ourselves, is dependent on the decisions we make. Wisdom is needed not only for our own sakes, but also for the sakes of those linked to us. This is the invitation Jesus offers us: to find a firm foundation for our lives, and build a place of peace and shelter for those we love. The man whose house fell with a great crash lost more than lodgings. He lost everything: for himself and for his family.

What appears at first reading to be a comic and perhaps trivial story reveals itself, on closer inspection, to be a piercing analysis of the human condition. We aspire to peace and prosperity – for ourselves and for those we love. We build

What to do

Structural survey: picture the life you have chosen to lead as a house, and survey it. Where are the structural weaknesses? What are the small sins that let the rain in through the roof in steady drips? Where you are shaky, is it because you have not sunk your foundations deep enough into Jesus?

Foundation analysis: face up to the question: is your life genuinely founded on Christ? Even if your immediate answer is 'Yes' – because you are a Christian – there is value in looking deeper, and asking again. It is in the substance of our lives that the foundation we choose will be seen. Think about the big decisions you make: career and lifestyle, relationships, money and spending. Is each of these areas of your life directly rooted in the wisdom and words of Jesus, or have you sought some other foundation? What might it take to reorientate the building of your life to Jesus as the one foundation?

Places to stay

In a world where many leaders are focused on their own self-enhancement, projected image and drives to control, Jesus teaches us another way. It is a way of being powerful when you are weak, tough when you're soft and huge when you are small. It is absolutely subversive of the model given to us by a self-besotted world. *Viv Thomas*[97]

We are glutted with information but we are starved for wisdom. We know so much about everything under the sun, but we live astonishingly trivial lives. Why? Why do we know so much and live so badly? Well, partly at least because we as a culture are admiring all the wrong people and have lost touch with the 'wise'. *Eugene Peterson*[98]

R E T R O - T O U R

Therefore whosoever heareth these sayings of mine, and doeth them, I will liken him unto a wise man, which built his house upon a rock: And the rain descended, and the floods came, and the winds blew, and beat upon that house; and it fell not: for it was founded upon a rock. And every one that heareth these sayings of mine, and doeth them not, shall be likened unto a foolish man, which built his house upon the sand: And the rain descended, and the floods came, and the winds blew, and beat upon that house; and it fell: and great was the fall of it.

our individual homes, and our homes are bolted together into communities. Our communities in turn form nations and empires, until the impact of our building spreads across the very face of the earth. But peace eludes us, because we do not have, at heart, the wisdom of God. Why is it after centuries of technological and economic development that over one billion people – one in five of the world's population – live in poverty? Because we do not have the right foundations. How is it that, according to reliable predictions, at the midpoint of the twenty-first century the economic losses attributable to global warming will exceed the total output of the world's economy? Because we do not have the right foundations. The tragedy of the human condition is that we lack the wisdom to build well.

This then, is what Jesus comes to offer – access to the deeper wisdom by which the lives we build, alone and together, will have the strength and substance to carry the shalom of God. The Sermon on the Mount is not a pocket guide to individual

salvation, nor the recipe book for cooking up a better religion. It is a blueprint for the human experiment, a manifesto for the life we were created to lead.

4. THE COMMON TOUCH

Location *Matthew 7:28-29*. When Jesus had finished saying these things, the crowds were amazed at his teaching, because he taught as one who had authority, and not as their teachers of the law.

Landmarks The 'inner authority of Jesus' – a different kind of power. The authenticity of Jesus – a man in touch with the human condition.

What to see The final credits have rolled, and are down to Third Assistant Key Grip. The film's closing music has given way to an additional track that has little to do with the plot, but will help soundtrack sales. The house lights slowly come up, as all over the cinema seats fold, coats are picked up and empty popcorn barrels are kicked aside. As you climb the gently sloping floor toward the exit, you overhear snatches of the conversations around you. Within a matter of moments, you have been able to assess the impact that the film has had. Is the audience filing out still trembling with shock and fear, or already repeating to one another the script's funniest one-liners? Were they totally taken by surprise when the final moment revealed whodunit? Is there some mystery

SUBWAY MAP

STATION
Job 28:28, Proverbs 3:19, Hosea 14:9 – the wisdom of God as the centrepiece of all we build.

CONNECTIONS
Romans 11:33, I Corinthians 1:25, James 1:5, James 3:7 – wisdom at work in our life with Christ.

DISTRICT 5: FRUITFUL

that, even at the end of two hours, they still cannot fathom, or some continuity error that has punctured the film's credibility entirely? One thing you can guarantee, as you mingle with the post-movie crowd, is that a whole series of instant reviews will be offered, and that the judgement viewers express within moments of the film's end will be, in all likelihood, the judgement they retain. I will never forget seeing my son come through the door just minutes after watching *The Blair Witch Project*. He looked, quite literally, as if he had seen a ghost.

If this represents a scene with which you are familiar, you might want to ask yourself how Matthew, and those on whose additional accounts he has relied to construct his account of the Sermon, knew what the audience were thinking. You can be sure that there wasn't a man leaping to his feet as soon as Jesus finished speaking to declare in a loud voice 'Behold, he speaks as one who has authority, and not as the teachers of the law'. Nor would there be the opportunity for a long panned shot of the crowd holding their hands to their heads and, wide-eyed, looking suitably amazed. What is far more likely is that Matthew and the eyewitnesses on whom he would later rely mingled with the crowd as they dispersed, and heard snatches and snippets of conversation. It was from these conversations that this single theme would emerge. Perhaps expressed in a hundred different ways, in reference to different areas and aspects of the

teaching, this one opinion rose to the surface – that whatever else you felt about Jesus, he had a natural authority. You can agree or disagree with his conclusions, but you cannot deny that this is a man worth listening to. Perhaps those who later became part of the church and were known to Matthew would also remember other conversations they had, over the evening meal or on the long walk home. From these conversations, too, this same theme would emerge: there is something different about Jesus. He is not just another religious teacher or run-of-the-mill travelling rabbi. There is value in the words he has shared with us.

The crowds are explicit in stating that the authority they see in Jesus is not the authority of the teachers of the law. This implies two things. Firstly that Jesus was not linked with the institutional authority of the Jewish faith. There is an authority that comes from holding power in a religious institution. It is an external, positional authority that has its place but can often be off-putting to ordinary people. Often it is more to do with power than with truth. Whatever it was that these people saw in Jesus, it was neither external nor positional. The authority he carried was an inner authority, which needed neither rank nor title to define it. Secondly, the crowd's reaction indicates that Jesus did not speak as a highbrow academic. The teachers of the law were the legal, moral, social and theological experts of their day. Some had studied day and night for decades, and they prided themselves on the breadth and depth of their knowledge. They had authority over the uneducated because they knew so many things that ordinary people did not know: they were the gatekeepers of the knowledge economy of their day. However Jesus came across to these crowds, he did not come across as a dry academic. Clearly he knew many things – the depth of his intellect leaps out at you from even a cursory reading of these words, but his knowledge did not seem to be divorced from the real world in the way that of some other teachers was – and is today.

Then as now, power and knowledge were the currency with which most leaders exercised authority over others. But here was a different kind of authority. It was an authority that didn't leave people battered and berated and newly aware of their inadequacy – but rather lifted their spirits with amazement and astonishment.

If I were to hazard a guess as to what it was in these teachings of Jesus that produced this reaction, I would use the word authenticity. This is a personal impression, but it does seem that the authority of these words is an authority with its feet firmly on the ground. The wisdom of Jesus is a wisdom that embraces the lives of common people, that stands with them in the sweat and grime of their compromised lives. Jesus manages, somehow, to share in the very ordinariness of life but at the same time to touch the divine. It is as if he takes a piece

of the realm of God – that holy place that is beyond our present understanding and to which we can only aspire – and brings it down to earth in our presence. He takes the dust of our lives in one hand and the dream of God in the other, and allows us to believe for a moment that the two can come together. The teaching of Jesus resonates with the realities of the lives we lead. He has authority because we know, deep within ourselves, that his description of our condition rings true.

My sense is that this is in essence the authority not of the Messiah, nor even of the Saviour, but of the Creator. Jesus stands before us on the mount that he himself made, breathing the air whose composition he derived and pointing out the trees whose fruitfulness was his suggestion. His prescription for human life rings true because humanity was his idea in the first place. He was there when half-formed shapes on a drawing board came together as arms and legs: when inspiration struck and the word human was first breathed. He knows us better than we know ourselves, and his teaching reveals the uncanny depth of his perception.

The teachers of the law could only ever be second-hand intellectuals. No matter how well they knew their subject, they could never enter in to its reality. Jesus, by contrast, is the subject. It's the difference between talking to a group of music critics and meeting Mozart; between taking the standard tour of the

What to do

Give thanks to God – for the rich wisdom of these words, for their authenticity and for the authority of the one who offers them.

Name before God – the things you have learned as you have journeyed through the Sermon on the Mount. Give thanks for each one, and renew your commitment to act on them in the great adventure that lies before you.

Pray – for the ongoing impact of these words upon our world. Pray that once more in our age the poor in spirit, the merciful, those who hunger and thirst might hear the wonderful news, that God is for them and has initiated the rescue plan of grace.

Places to stay

So, God speaks to us through the world around us. All the beauty that I see in creation must in some way be in him who made it. We should strive to think of him in new ways, we should try to break out of our stereotyped manner of speaking with him. Perhaps we should address him as "the One who makes the rainbows', or as 'the One who listens to the hills', and thus begin to form a new picture of awe and beauty to replace our dull and faded images. *Ian Petit*[99]

It would be strange indeed to collect all kinds of data about the human experience, and yet not take time to weight up the claims of Jesus which many people have found make sense of everything else. This is what it is all about. This is the ultimate meaning of humankind. *John Allan*[100]

R E T R O - T O U R

And it came to pass, when Jesus had ended these sayings, the people were astonished at his doctrine: For he taught them as one having authority, and not as the scribes.

Louvre that stops off at the Mona Lisa, and having a special one-on-one with Leonardo.

The outcome of authenticity is trust. Because this is a man whose authority is real and unforced, this is a man who can be trusted. Perhaps the most exhilarating aspect of these words collected for us as the Sermon on the Mount is that there were those in the crowd – most of them hearing Jesus for the first time – who later made the choice to trust and became his followers. Without doubt at least some of the 120 who gathered on the day of Pentecost, and the three thousand who within hours had joined them, were present to hear this teaching for the first time. The deep impact it had on them, and the extent to which their lives were changed is evidenced in the very fact that we have these words today. They were memorised, passed on and ultimately recorded not because of their eloquence or beauty, but because they changed lives. It was the reality, not the rhetoric of the Sermon on the Mount that ensured its survival.

SUBWAY MAP

STATION
Isaiah 11:1-5 – the inner authority of the promised Messiah.

CONNECTIONS
Luke 2:40, Matthew 13:54, I Corinthians 1:24, Colossians 2:3 – the wisdom of Jesus in his childhood, in his teaching and in his church.

References

1 Quoted in Colin Chapman, *Shadows of the Supernatural*, (Oxford: Lion, 1990), p69

2 Mark Honan, *Switzerland*, (Victoria: Lonely Planet Publications, 2000), p14

3 Calver, Chilcraft, Meadows, Morris, *Uncage the Lion, Spring Harvest Seminar Notes*, (Uckfield: Spring Harvest, 1990), p39

4 Matthew 5:1-7,29; 10:5-42; 13:1-52 and 18:1-35.

5 Luke 9:2-5; 10:3; 21:12-17 [12:11-12 ; 6:40 ; 12:2-9] [12:51-53; 14:25-27] [17:33 ; 10:16]

6 Quoted in Jeff Lucas, *A Royal Banquet, Spring Harvest Study Guide*, (Uckfield: Spring Harvest, 2000), p40

7 Quoted in J.M. and M.J. Cohen, *The Penguin Book of Modern Quotations*, (London: Penguin, 1971), p121

8 Richard Foster, *Money, Sex and Power: The challenge to the disciplined life*, (London: Hodder and Stoughton, 1985), pp1-15

9 Richard Foster, *Money, Sex and Power: The challenge to the disciplined life* (London: Hodder and Stoughton, 1985), p3

10 Viv Thomas, *Future Leader*, (Carlisle: Paternoster, 1999), p3

11 Mike Riddell, *Godzone – A Guide to the Travels of the Soul*, (Oxford: Lion, 1992), p37

12 Quoted in J.M and M.J. Cohen, *The Penguin Dictionary of Modern Quotations*, (London: Penguin, 1971), p137

13 Quoted in J.M. and M.J. Cohen, *The Penguin Dictionary of Modern Quotations*, (London: Penguin, 1971), p338

14 Tony Campolo with Gordon Aeschliman, *50 Ways you can help save the planet* (Eastbourne: Kingsway, 1993), p10

15 Walter Brueggemann, *The Prophetic Imagination* (Philadelphia: Fortress Press, 1978), p13

16 Richard Wurmbrand, *Tortured for Christ, 30th Anniversary Edition*, (Bartlesville: Living Sacrifice Book C, 1998), pp76 and 86

17 From *With Burning Hearts*, quoted in Viv Thomas, *Second Choice*, (Carlisle: Paternoster, 2000), p12

18 Quoted in John Blanchard, *Gathered Gold*, (Welwyn: Evangelical Press, 1984), p11

19 Genesis 1:28

20 See, for instance Numbers 18:19 and 2 Chronicles 13:5

21 John R.W. Stott, *Christian Counter-Culture*, (Leicester, IVP, 1978), p60

22 Luke 18:27

23 Quoted in Calver, Chilcraft and Meadows, *Beyond Belief, Spring Harvest Main Seminar Notes*, (Uckfield: Spring Harvest, 1996), p12

24 Abraham Kuyper, *Lectures on Calvinism*, (Michigan: Eerdmans, 1987)

25 Carlo Carretto, *Letters from the Desert*, (London: Darton, Longman and Todd 1972), p40

26 D.A. Carson, *Jesus' Sermon on the Mount*, (Carlisle: Global Christian Publishers, 1999), p32

27 D.A. Carson, *Jesus' Sermon on the Mount*, (Carlisle: Global Christian Publishers, 1999), p32

28 Quoted in Jeff Lucas, *A Royal Banquet, Spring Harvest Study Guide*, (Uckfield: Spring Harvest, 2000), p18

29 Hans Kung, *Why Priests*, (Glasgow: Collins, 1972), p14

30 Dewi Hughes with Matthew Bennett, *God of the Poor*, (Carlisle: Paternoster, 1998), p56

31 John R.W. Stott, *The Meaning of the Sermon on the Mount*, (Leicester: IVP, 1978), p75

32 Quoted in Charles R Swindoll, *The Grace Awakening*, (Milton Keynes: Word UK, 1990), p82

33 Quoted in Calver, Chilcraft and Meadows, *Beyond Belief, Spring Harvest Main Seminar Notes*, (Uckfield: Spring Harvest, 1996), p8

34 Genesis 4:8

35 Quoted in Johann Christoph Arnold, *The Lost Art of Forgiving*, (Robertsbridge: The Plough Publishing House, 1998), p32

36 Quoted in Calver, Chilcraft and Meadows, *Beyond Belief, Spring Harvest Main Seminar Notes*, (Uckfield: Spring Harvest, 1996), p98

37 C.S. Lewis, *Mere Christianity*, quoted in Richard Foster, *Money, Sex and Power*, (London: Hodder and Stoughton, 1985), p103

38 Richard Foster, *Money, Sex and Power*, (London: Hodder and Stoughton, 1985), p99

39 In the foreword to Viv Thomas, *Second Choice*, (Carlisle, Paternoster, 2000), pxii

40 John R.W. Stott, *Christian Counter-Culture*, (Leicester, IVP, 1978), p92

41 Quoted in Richard Foster, *Money, Sex and Power*, (London: Hodder and Stoughton, 1985), p150

42 Joan Winmill Brown, Editor, *The Martyred Christian: 160 Readings from Dietrich Bonhoeffer*, (New York: Collier/Macmillan, 1983), p107

43 Exodus 21:22-25, Leviticus 24:19 and Deuteronomy 19:21

44 Martin Luther King, *Strength to Love*, (London: Fontana Religious, 1963), p54

45 Literally 'satyagraha'. See John R.W. Stott, *Christian Counter-Culture*, (Leicester, IVP, 1978), p109

46 Hans Kung, *Why Priests*, (Glasgow: Collins, 1972), p18

47 Aleksandr Solzhenitsyn, *The First Circle*, quoted in J.M. and M.J. Cohen, *The Penguin Dictionary of Modern Quotations*, (London: Penguin, 1971), p312

48 Gordon Bailey, *Stuff and Nonsense: A Collection of Verse and Worse*, (Oxford: Lion, 1989), p44

49 Philip Yancey, *The Jesus I Never Knew*, (London: Harper Collins, 1995), p140-142

50 Philip Yancey, *The Jesus I Never Knew*, (London: Harper Collins, 1995), p141

51 David Adam, *Power Lines: Celtic Prayers About Work*, (London: Triangle, 1992), p57

52 Gordon Bailey, *Stuff and Nonsense: A Collection of Verse and Worse*, Oxford: Lion, 1989), p93

53 Philip Yancey, *The Jesus I Never Knew*, (London: Harper Collins, 1995), p142

54 A phrase of Dietrich Bonhoeffer

55 Quoted in Caitlin Matthews, *The Little Book of Celtic Blessings*, (Shaftesbury: Element Books, 1994), p14

56 Quoted in Calver, Chilcraft and Meadows, *Beyond Belief, Spring Harvest Main Seminar Notes*, (Uckfield: Spring Harvest, 1996), p76

57 Carlo Carretto, *Letters from the Desert*, (London: Darton, Longman and Todd, 1972), pxvii

58 Carlo Carretto, *Love is for Living*, translated by Jeremy Moiser, (London: Darton, Longman and Todd 1976), p12

59 Carlo Carretto, *Letters from the Desert*, (London: Darton, Longman and Todd, 1972), pxix

60 Carlo Carretto, *Letters from the Desert*, (London: Darton, Longman and Todd, 1972), pxx

61 Dallas Willard, *The Divine Conspiracy: Redisovering our Hidden Life in God*, (London: Harper Collins, 1998), p393

62 Richard Foster, *Money, Sex and Power: The challenge to the disciplined life*, (London: Hodder and Stoughton, 1985), p123

63 Thomas à Kempis, *The Imitation of Christ*, [Book 1 Ch. 20]

64 Quoted in Jeff Lucas, *A Royal Banquet, Spring Harvest Study Guide*, (Uckfield: Spring Harvest, 2000), p82

65 Exodus 4:22-23

66 Revelation 21:2-3

67 Tom Wright, *The Lord and His Prayer*, (London: Triangle, 1996), p2

68 Quoted in John Blanchard, *Gathered Gold*, (Welwyn: Evangelical Press, 1984), p1

69 Ephesians 4:26

70 Verses 14-15

71 Quoted in Johann Christoph Arnold, *The Lost Art of Forgiving*, (Robertsbridge: The Plough Publishing House, 1998), pxii

72 Ephesians 4:27

73 Tom Wright, *The Lord and His Prayer*, (London: Triangle, 1996), p63

74 Quoted in Johann Christoph Arnold, *The Lost Art of Forgiving*, (Robertsbridge: The Plough Publishing House, 1998), p100

75 Luke 10:25-37

76 Tom Wright, *The Lord and His Prayer*, (London: Triangle, 1996), p22

77 Ronald Rolheiser, *The Shattered Lantern: Rediscovering the Felt Presence of God*, (London: Hodder and Stoughton, 1994), p170

78 Quoted in Jeff Lucas, *A Royal Banquet, Spring Harvest Study Guide*, (Uckfield: Spring Harvest, 2000), p80

79 Adapted from John Blanchard, *Gathered Gold*, (Welwyn: Evangelical Press, 1984), p259

80 Juliet Schor, *The Overspent American: Upscaling, Downshifting, and the New Consumer*, Basic Books, 1998, Quoted by John R. Mueller, re:generation quarterly, Volume 4, Number 4

81 Alister Maclean, *Hebridean Altars*, Quoted in Caitlin Matthews, *The Little Book of Celtic Blessings*, (Shaftesbury: Element Books, 1994), p23

82 Huton Smith, *Beyond the Post-modern Mind*, (New York: Crossroads, 1982), p191

83 Quoted in John Blanchard, *Gathered Gold*, (Welwyn: Evangelical Press, 1984), p6

84 de Caussade, Jean-Pierre, *Spiritual Letters of Jean-Pierre de Caussade*, translated by Kitty Muggeridge, (London: Fount Paperbacks, 1986), p84-5

85 Quoted in Charles R Swindoll, *The Grace Awakening*, (Milton Keynes: Word UK, 1990), p94

86 Ronald Rolheiser, *The Shattered Lantern: Rediscovering the Felt Presence of God*, (London: Hodder and Stoughton, 1994), p107

87 Carlo Carretto, *Letters from the Desert*, (London: Darton, Longman and Todd, 1972), p40

88 Quoted in Kitty Muggeridge, *Gazing on Truth: Meditations on Reality*, (London: Triangle, 1985), p39

89 Luke 18:25

90 Mike Riddell, *Godzone – A Guide to the Travels of the Soul*, (Oxford: Lion, 1992), p39

91 Kitty Muggeridge, *Gazing on Truth: Meditations on Reality*, (London: Triangle, 1985), p12

92 Viv Thomas, *Future Leader*, (Carlisle: Paternoster, 1999), p23

93 Mother Mary Clare, SLG, *Encountering the Depths*, quoted in Josephine Bax, *The Good Wine: Spiritual Renewal in the Church of England*, (London: Church House Publishing, 1986), p55

94 Acts 19:13-16

95 Mike Riddell, *Godzone – A Guide to the Travels of the Soul*, (Oxford: Lion, 1992), 19

96 Robert E Webber, *Ancient-Future Faith: Rethinking Evangelicalism for a Postmodern World*, (Grand Rapids, Michigan: Baker Books, 1999), p83

97 Viv Thomas, *Future Leader*, (Carlisle: Paternoster, 1999), p176

98 In the foreword to Viv Thomas, *Second Choice*, (Carlisle, Paternoster, 2000), pxii

99 Ian Petit, *The God Who Speaks*, (London: Darton, Longman and Todd, 1989), p77

100 John Allan, *The Human Difference*, (Oxford: Lion, 1989), p156